TAKING OFF

How To Be Paid To Travel

Global Publishing Group
Australia • New Zealand • Singapore • America • London

PRAISE FOR THE AUTHOR

"Thank you so much for your time yesterday. You made me feel safe, comfortable and confident and it was a real pleasure talking to you. Thank you for your generosity with your time and wisdom. After seeing you I really did feel a change in my perspective on a number of issues and felt motivated to take some positive action as a result!"

– Cath Hopkin, Lawyer

"Your presentation skills are second to none."

– Lorraine Garvie, CEO District 32, Scotland.

"It was lovely speaking with you today! You really inspire me with the way you lead your life!"

– Deb Sonenberg, Artist & Theatre Director.

"Loved you're energy today – great presentation!"

– Daniel Reid, Director, Emanate Finance, Australia

"Your talk was amazing and really felt relevant to what is happening in my life right now!"

– Tracey Regan, Lemon Tree Books

"You were very easy to listen to and very engaging."

– Lita Squibb, Midas Bookkeeping

"You were great! Loved listening to you."

– Melinda Brennan, Public Speaker & Coach

"I hope all is going well with you and your book/business/love and the fabulous life that you lead. I am very thankful for the time I had with you and the inspiration from who you are as a person."

– Angela Mulligan USA, Coach.

"Thank you very much for your beautiful email, it made me realise how wonderful it is for us to fully take charge of our lives. Not expecting anyone else to drive it, but taking responsibility for the things that happen, that we attract. So empowering! I love it!"

– Catherine Fewings MBA

Taking Off **is an inspirational exploration of how to navigate life. The lessons shared in this book are just the beginning of what is a life long journey of self-discovery to success.**

Here's what people are saying about this book:

"Thank you for the privilege of reading your book. I have read up to chapter six in one sitting WOW what an amazing read on so many levels!"

– T. Tehan, Melbourne

"Fascinating to read the interviews, their journeys, their ways of dealing, striving their successes and non-successes!"

"Love the quotes!" – Deb Sonenberg, Melbourne

"On a personal level this is exactly the book I should be reading right now... and I think everyone is going to think that while they are reading this.... It will speak to each person at whatever stage of their own personal journey!"

– Tania T

"Just brilliant...well done!" – Miss Daymond Designs, Australia

TAKING OFF

How To Be Paid To Travel

MERRIAN STYLES

DISCLAIMER

All the information, techniques, skills and concepts contained within this publication are of the nature of general comment only and are not in any way recommended as individual advice. The intent is to offer a variety of information to provide a wider range of choices now and in the future, recognising that we all have widely diverse circumstances and viewpoints. Should any reader choose to make use of the information contained herein, this is their decision, and the contributors (and their companies), authors and publishers do not assume any responsibilities whatsoever under any condition or circumstances. It is recommended that the reader obtain their own independent advice.

First Edition 2019

National Library of Australia

Cataloguing-in-Publication entry:

Creator: Styles, Merrian, author.

Title: Taking Off : How To Be Paid To Travel / Merrian Styles.

ISBN: 9781925288704 (paperback)

Subjects: Travel.

Travel--Economic aspects.

Travelers--Finance, Personal.

Published by Global Publishing Group

PO Box 517 Mt Evelyn, Victoria 3796 Australia

Email info@GlobalPublishingGroup.com.au

For further information about orders:

Phone: +61 3 9726 4133 or Fax +61 3 8648 6871

I dedicate this book to those brave individuals
who have the courage to take that leap of faith,
to explore the world and all it has to offer,
with an open heart and an open mind.

Merrian Styles

Get a **FREE** copy of these books by Merrian Styles ...

The Easy Guide to Everything Quantum

3 Easy Steps to Instant Success with Positive Affirmations

... with any

BONUS OFFER

purchase!

BONUS OFFER 1 **$47.00**

Six PACK of audio recordings of original interviews with:

- Natasha Zuvela, Confidence on Camera
- Dr John Demartini, Human Behaviour Specialist
- Mark Cowne, CEO Kruger Cowne
- Cyndi O'Meara, Changing Habits, Changing Lives
- Graham (Skroo) Turner, CEO Flight Centre Group
- Karl E Watkin MBE, British Businessman of the Year

BONUS OFFER 2 **$97.00**

Trilogy pack: A three part home study course

- Values and Passion test
- Overcoming Objections
- Road to success

BONUS OFFER 3 **$497.00**

Fun, seven-part home study series:

1. Flight preparation
   - What you need to know
2. Checklist – What you need to ask
3. Prepare for take-off
   - Why are you in a holding pattern?
4. Full throttle and lift off
   - How you shift gears and rev up!
5. Inflight entertainment – Why you need fun
6. Prepare for landing – How to make adjustments
7. Touch down – The adventure begins!

... plus **FREE** Top Ten Survival Tips (e-book) by Merrian Styles

For a Media Kit or more information

Email: info@merrianstyles.com or visit **www.MerrianStyles.com**

ACKNOWLEDGEMENTS

There are so many people that I have to thank starting with my family. If it weren't for the courage and love of my two beautiful daughters, Aja and Justine, I would not have made it this far. To their father, Stephen, for sharing a life filled with adventures that took us to faraway places around the globe. To Andrew and Grace, the newest members of the team thank you for coming into our lives.

To my mentors and teachers, Dr John Demartini, Ben Harvey, Deepak Chopra, Panache Desi, Claire Zammit, Katherine Woodward Thomas, Christie Marie Sheldon, John Assaraf, Burt Goldman, Vishen Lakhiani and Jeffrey Slayter who introduced me to Darren J. Stephens.

To my lifelong friends Annie and Bill Fox who created the space for me to take this journey. To Helen Hope author, astrologer and friend who guided me with loving care during my early days in Singapore. To Deb Sonenberg, whose loving support and friendship nourished me through the drought years. To Vicki de Vauno and Heather (Scott) Thelwell together we navigated the good and the bad, sharing the wine, the tears and the laughter.

To my tribe of women who share the same ethos, are travelling a similar path, all of whom are lovingly nurturing and supporting each other along the way. Jeanette Hamilton, Megan Clarke, Catherine Fewings and Andrea (Keil) Marslen.

To the Feminine Power Sisterhood and my evolutionary sisters for all your loving support. To Robyn Ama'taria Creighton, for guiding me to Awaken Mentally.

To my Gym Girls, who saw me through the dark days of divorce. Lee Pinner, Terri Ludovico, Annette Rutherford, Helen Morris, Lee Barlow, Maria Palermo, Olly Armitage, Toni Frank and Tania Rose.

To Roger Ballard, Naomi Bickley and Beth Hender, an extraordinary trio, without you I would not have learned to silence my mind and uncover the treasures within. Also to Wendy Peak for meditation group which helped me in the early years of going solo without feeling alone.

To all my fellow expat friends and travellers I met along the way, too many to mention. You know who you are.

Thank you to Gareth Lane and my marketing team at Concise Digital, Suresh Babu, Abilash Praveen, Tammy Brown and Chris Gill.

Lastly, a special thank you to the team at Global Publishing. Thank you to Darren J. Stephens for taking me on this incredible adventure. To the wonderful Helen Busse, Kelly Mayne and the rest of the crew in Melbourne.

My heart felt gratitude and appreciation for you all.

Merrian Styles

CONTENTS

INTRODUCTION

How can I be paid to travel? This was the question I asked myself as I sat in the hotel seminar room along with forty other people all working away at their values.

Two weeks earlier I had attended the Breakthrough Experience with Dr John Demartini. John spoke about how our values affect every area of our lives if we take the time and trouble to look.

There I sat examining my life, looking for the evidence he assured me my life would show me, and then I saw it! The light bulb went on. Oh my God! It was there right in front of me and I'd never been aware of it before. It felt like I'd found the code that made the enigma machine work and all the pieces dropped into place!

Travel was my highest value, my home reflected it, as I'd collected art and treasures from every country I had lived in, over the past 25 years. What was really shocking was the realisation that I had chosen my life partner based on my highest value too. Well he made me an offer I couldn't turn down. A life filled with adventure and travel! How could I say no?

Understanding there are many ways you can be paid to travel I decided to seek out experts in their fields, all being paid to travel, and ask them about their journeys. Why travel is important to them, what their journeys looked like with a view to uncovering our common denominators. What was it that we all shared that would help others to follow their dreams and be paid to travel?

What unfolds in the following chapters is a passion for what we do, the perseverance to see it through. An unrelenting self-belief, that everything is possible, a bravery and courage to get out of our comfort zones and take those leaps of faith.

To be an inspiration to the generations to come should be the common goal of all mankind. But taking inspiration from others is a vital step in that goal. In a letter to his 25-year-old self, Sir Richard Branson told himself:

"Let your dreams guide your path. Don't let the naysayers deter you. Screw business as usual and do things your own way. Your ability to take calculated risks and your incurable optimism will lead to great heights – both in business and in life."

Taking Off offers both the inspiration and helpful advice to those, who want to follow their dreams, expand their horizons and embrace what life has to offer whilst getting paid to do what they love.

Everything is possible.

CHAPTER ONE

Well-oiled Solutions

Merrian Styles

World Traveller, Consultant, Author and Speaker

"Being a minnow in an ocean of sharks takes courage and fosters an agility to move quickly, And know when it's time to get out"

Merrian Styles

CHAPTER ONE

Well-oiled Solutions

Merrian Styles
World Traveller, Consultant, Author and Speaker

Scuba diving off the coast of Sharm El Sheik, in the crystal clear blue water of the Red Sea it was hard to imagine my life was soon to change forever. My husband and I had started our partnership in Israel in 1978. At that time the Israelis held occupied Egyptian territory. I recall thinking, strange that three decades later I find myself back here in the Sinai, back where it all started. It was as if I'd come full circle, back to the beginning of my life of travel and adventure.

I have always loved the John Donne quote:

> *"Thy firmness makes my circle just, and makes me end where I begun."*

In January 2011 freshly returned from two years of living in Cairo, my re-entry back into Australia was bumpy to say the least. Cairo had erupted in civil unrest, which eventually saw the downfall of President Mubarak and what is now known as the Arab Spring Uprising. It was a timely exit, and felt as though the unrest came home with us in the luggage. Those first six weeks after we returned were turbulent.

Biggest Impact on my Life

We'd come back to a very different environment to the one we left. Work was no longer plentiful, everyone we knew was looking for contracts and our home was overcrowded with the furniture of two households, with more arriving from Cairo.

Our daughters had come home to join us for the festive season. We hadn't seen them since the Christmas before, when they had joined us in Cairo for a cruise down the Nile. Happy family reunion was my agenda, sadly it wasn't their father's or so it seemed. The stress of returning to this new economic climate, was taking its toll. The strain of several years of my husband's family disputes in UK, and the grief of losing his father and mother in quick succession under unhappy circumstances proved too much to bear for him and for us.

During those six weeks, my husband's erratic behaviour worsened. Far from celebration, it was more like living over a minefield, never certain when you might put a foot out of place with explosive consequences. The girls and I were all afraid the slightest thing would set him off, he was primed and ready to blow. And blow he did. The fuse that set him off was my asking, when was he planning to go back to UK to sort out his UK family's matters? He'd been avoiding this task for over two years. His response was immediate and violent.

By the end of January it was clear that something had to give. It was agreed he would return to UK to sort out the UK family matters alone. Growing up in a British boarding school he hated 'goodbyes' so we agreed never to use the word, even though there were frequent times we spent apart.

For the first time in over thirty years I said "goodbye" to my husband. I watched as the realisation and import of what I had said sunk in. I can still see his astonished face in the rear vision mirror as I drove away. I put him on a plane bound for UK, changed the locks on the house and said get some help or don't come back. I'd pulled the pin on the grenade, which shattered our family and our business. My life as I'd known it was over.

The Lows

Weeks later, still finding myself huddled on the floor of the shower sobbing, in a brave effort to convince myself otherwise, I progressed to singing the James Brown song "I feel good, I knew that I would, " as I let the water cascade over me looking for the courage to face another day. Clearly I felt anything but good!

It was just such a morning that a sobering thought occurred to me. I was no longer a wife, no longer a mother as the girls had grown up and moved interstate, no longer a company director and no longer employed. My marriage and business partnership were over. Time to ask some tough questions. Who am I?

> *"A woman is like a tea bag – you can't tell how strong she is until you put her in hot water."*
>
> **Eleanor Roosevelt**

As often happens for women in partnerships, we disappear. We are no longer ourselves instead we become, someone's partner, wife, or mother. No longer the young girl with big dreams of travelling the world. I had succeeded in that. What was I going to do now? It was clear, that to continue as business partners would not work. Where to next, I asked?

What followed were weeks of psychology sessions, in an attempt to make it through the next day. Taking one day at a time, exchanging

emails like tossing grenades, doing battle over property and trying to unravel all we had built up over thirty years was harrowing. It took a couple of years and a lot of soul searching, when the answer came to me.

Find a way to be paid to travel again!

The Dream

My love of travel stemmed from my discovery of books at the early age of around seven. My third-grade teacher introduced me to the local public library. There I met and fell in love with my first Frenchman, Anatole of Paris. Anatole was a small mouse, with big dreams, living in the sewers of Paris.

Anatole dreamed of travelling to faraway places like Istanbul, London and Rome. These were dreams I shared and together we went on many adventures. Of course all the other mice laughed and mocked Anatole and said how could a small mouse like you travel the world? But quietly and determinedly Anatole set out a plan to make his adventures a reality.

Not surprisingly when I was asked what I wanted to do when I grew up and replied,

> *"I want to travel the world, live overseas and have lots of adventures!"*

I too was laughed at and it was suggested to me that hairdressing or nursing would be a better ambition.

Despite all the laughter and ridicule, I followed Anatole's example. I kept my plans to myself, shared a vision that was acceptable to family and friends, and determinedly held on to my dreams and at the first opportunity, aged 18, got my first passport and headed to Europe.

The Proposal

After Europe and a failed start at academic life in Canberra, I found myself back in Sydney, working as an article clerk at a North Sydney firm and studying Law at Sydney University. My days were filled with property settlements and the occasional unpleasant divorce.

My dream of travel was never far from the surface, and I had islands on my mind, so I determined to make a break for it, and head to Bali with a girlfriend. Sadly my plans had to change and instead I found myself travelling solo to Brampton Island off the coast of Queensland. It was not the adventure I planned, but it was an island.

On arriving on Brampton, seated at the other end of the breakfast table was a handsome Englishman who would shape my life and my destiny in ways I could not imagine. It was a summer holiday romance, or so I thought and when the week was up, I headed back to my desk in North Sydney.

A week later the Englishman phoned to say the land rig he was working on was moving and he had some time off and was driving to Sydney to see me. Four days later he arrived, astonished at the size of Australia, measuring his progress in inches on the map as each day passed. In Europe he would have arrived in Turkey by then.

We spent six glorious weeks together before he was heading back to Singapore when me made me an offer I couldn't refuse. The proposal went something like this:

"I don't know what I can offer you except a life that will never be dull and boring, filled with adventure and travel." To which I promptly replied, "When do we leave?"

One Saturday in April the following year we were married. I'd only known him for six months and we had only spent six week together in that time. On the following Monday, I found myself back at my desk in the law firm, wondering if it had all been a dream.

First Adventure

Another three months passed before I saw him again. By then I'd handed in my resignation and headed once more to London. After we were married, he had changed jobs, applied to become a mud engineer and was sent to Houston for training. He left me as a long-haired hippy backpacker who had been tossed out of University, sold his motor bike to buy a one way ticket to Singapore and returned from the States, a clean shaven, denim suit wearing someone his mother didn't even recognise! What had I done, I asked myself?

Our first posting was to Israel working in the Sinai, for a bogus corporation set up by the service company which didn't want their Arab customers to know they were busily exploring the Sinai for oil. Our El Al flight was three hours late; the thinking was, if there was a bomb on board it would blow up before we left the tarmac. Everything we carried was examined, including me stripped down to my underwear. Security suddenly became a high priority.

As the designated money manager of this joint enterprise, my job entailed trying to get hold of some of the stuff – money that is. No easy task as wage cheques took weeks to get to us in Tel Aviv, and another six weeks for the banks to cash. No online banking, no mobile phones back then. How were we supposed to eat in the meantime? I needed to **find another way**. This was the beginning of the development of my enterprising skills, born out of necessity.

The answer was Norman's bar. Norman was a British expat who owned a local bar and offered a cheque exchange service for a percentage cut. This worked well for Norman as most of the money was spent in the bar the same night. Tel Aviv was a party town. Most of the population aged in their twenties, like us, were in the army, wearing fatigues and facing the prospect of potential death each day. Which spelt PARTY!

The second part of getting paid involved me taking what was left of the US dollars down to the local market sitting drinking Arabic coffee and waiting for a buyer for my dollars. Some days it took all morning. I learnt quickly how to bargain before relinquishing my highly prized American dollars for less desirable Israeli pounds.

Safety and Security

One Saturday morning, I got news an expat riding a motorbike on the Sabbath had been beheaded riding down the street. A wire had been stretched across the street in an orthodox part of the city and took off his head. This new life of travel had its challenges. I decided I needed to keep my wits about me, and my head firmly on my shoulders.

One of the ways I safeguard against being caught in a country potentially being bombed, experiencing civil unrest or generally unsafe, is to always wear a 18-carat-gold chain I bought in Saudi Arabia. Gold has a universal value and is widely accepted, I decided I could bargain with gold, or use it to buy a ticket out if necessary. Thankfully I have never needed to use it, but there is safety in having a strategy in place to cover such events.

Years later an expat friend was seen on the international news, jumping from a plane escaping a hostage situation onto the runway. I have in the past bargained away watches, and I am always prepared to give up the

goods in exchange for an escape route, or a safe haven, as it seems to me to be a small price to pay for your freedom. I love to have a Plan B and highly recommend you do too.

First Company

In 1995, I set up our first company. I'd watched and learnt how this oil business worked and I could see that working for service companies was not the place to be. The money was working for the oil companies and the best way to do that was as a contractor.

My husband had established himself as a valuable employee and engineer. One day I sat him down and worked out the number of hours he worked in return for the pay he was getting and told him he'd earn more working at Woolworths stacking shelves. **There had to be a better way.** I knew what the oil company was paying for his services. I just needed a way to get paid direct, and cut out the middleman. The best way to do that was to set up our own company.

I'd been working for a not for profit organisation as an Executive Director which was great training in corporate compliance, I was answerable to a board of directors, so it was an easy transition for me to apply all I'd learned there to setting up our own company. What did we have to lose, I argued. Worst-case scenario, we lose our house if we can't make the mortgage payments, the best-case scenario we triple our income.

We tripled our income in the first twelve months. And doubled that again.

Biggest Achievement

Over the next 20 years our income grew steadily when another opportunity presented itself. Chevron was developing the Barrow Island Project off the coast of Western Australia and needed a mobile mud plant. There wasn't one in the southern hemisphere. One would need to be built, it was just a question of who would build and supply it.

The seat at the Chevron table had been offered to our company, however my husband was tied up with another contract at the time, so we filled the contract using another engineer. He came to me and proposed I build the plant, as he couldn't as it was a conflict of interest, so armed with drawings supplied by my husband, off I went first to the banks to get the finance to build the plant, costing around $650,000, then created a new company, then on to Vietnam and Singapore to source the people with the capability to construct and deliver the plant on time.

Once built and delivered, as luck would have it, the drilling on Barrow Island was hit by five cyclones, setting the project back by five months. Turning what was meant to be a four-month contract into a nine-month one and earning the company $1,100,000 in fees and transport cost recovery. At the end of the project our net profit was $250,000 in less than 18 months total turnaround time. It was a great result.

Benefits and Rewards

My passion for travel led me to find a partner who shared my passion for adventure. We also shared complementary skills. On the one side was chemical engineering, and the other, financial management and corporate compliance, the combination allowed us to seek contracts all over the world, wherever there was a project being proposed to explore for oil or gas. We travelled the world for over 25 years. Our unique combination meant, we got to pick and choose our contracts and places we wanted to live, and reject those we didn't.

We had two beautiful daughters together, both born overseas and both with a wanderlust and love of travel. My dream came true and so can yours.

It wasn't all easy. Each time we moved it would be like starting again. Another new place, I needed to source skilled workers, doctors, dentists, hairdressers and supermarkets. I needed to ask: Where can I buy good quality fresh produce? Find reliable maids, cooks, drivers and local staff? The first twelve months in each place is hard work. The second year is much easier. You just get settled and into a rhythm and it is time to move again.

Not Everywhere is Eden

There's a saying in the oil and gas business, never a 'stan', meaning if you have a choice never choose to go to Kazakhstan, Uzbekistan, or any place ending in 'stan'. They would not be on your bucket list of places to visit, so why work there if you have a choice?

Living and working somewhere is a very different experience to visiting on holiday with a fixed time frame and specific things to see. Living the experience means fitting in with the local population. Learning what is culturally appropriate and what is not.

Working as a contractor, you have to be aware of the political climate and how stable the situation is, going in. When operating outside of the oil company you don't have the same protection and often not the same support. Once you are there it may be difficult getting out. Remember my recommendation to have a Plan B.

Important Questions to Ask Wherever You Find Yourself Living

- Ask when religious and cultural days and events are happening. Don't get caught short with all shops shut for a week because it's Eid, Diwali, or Yom Kippur! This happened to me I ate the only food I could buy, pita bread filled with salad and falafel for days!

- Treat the humblest abode as if it is a palace. To the person who lives there it's their castle.

- Ask yourself, how can I fit in within the community? Blending in is better than standing out. When you stand out you can become a target for unwelcome attention.

- Ask how can I show respect? Perhaps by learning some of the local language, or obeying religious customs even if they are not your own.

- Ask what is polite behaviour and what is not.

- Ask what is acceptable clothing and what is not. Show respect for local customs.

- Ask what is important to the locals, where is there a need and do that. It could be helping out in the local school, hospital or a local charity.

- Give lots of praise and appreciation to all you see around you. The locals may never have travelled outside their town or city and will be looking for your approval as a world traveller.

- Show your gratitude and appreciation by offering your support to a local group or simply make sure everyone nearby has food to eat by sharing what is cooked in your kitchen with neighbours and your staff. It will be greatly appreciated and you will be loved for it.

Five Ps

I am often asked to summarise the lessons and takeaway's I've learned from living this expat life and from the various celebrities I interview. There are variations in each interview, as you will find when you read on, however I feel the following five Ps gives a general summary:

- Passion
- Perseverance
- Presence
- Participation
- Performance

If you do what you are **passionate** about your enthusiasm is contagious. People hear it in your voice and respond to it and what follows is success. Love what you do and you will be rewarded and it doesn't matter how obscure it seems, in fact the more niche it is, the greater the likelihood you will be paid handsomely, because there are fewer people out there offering the same services.

You need **perseverance**. You cannot go into it half-hearted. You must give it 110% if it's going to work. There were many times throughout the 25 years when giving up would have been an easy option. Had I given up I would have found myself living a suburban life living alongside my parents in the western suburbs of Sydney. I am not knocking that, if it's what your heart desires, it's just that was not for me. Giving up is never an option. You have to have perseverance.

Presence is a curious thing. What I mean by presence is being wholly present when you are dealing with people. Listening to them as though every word they speak is vital to your existence and survival. There is a chance it might be, if you miss some vital piece of information, everything could very easily go to hell very quickly. Misunderstandings can be avoided if you learn to be present with people and learn to actively listen and learn from them.

Participation. Get involved in your business, with your staff and also with the local community. I recall arriving in Cairo in 2008, direct from India. Luckily someone I knew in Chennai had lived in Cairo and forwarded me the details of the British woman who ran the Maadi British Association. On arrival, I had plans in place, to meet her the next day, to socialise with the local expats and to tap into the wealth of information they had to share. No point reinventing the wheel.

If you want to be successful, you need to dive right in. The oil company arranged for us to stay at the Intercontinental Hotel in Heliopolis until we found suitable accommodation. When I arrived I was greeted by a Canadian woman who had been holed up in the hotel for the past month too frightened to go outside. I took her by the hand and said come with me. It takes courage to dive into the unknown and it's not for everyone.

> *"Be prepared to get out of your comfort zone and into your courage zone."*
>
> **Merrian Styles**

Performance. No point doing something unless you do it well. And by doing it well you will always be asked back or sent forward into the next adventure. I can cite several times where people didn't thrive and it's not indicative of race or creed. One example was an Indian engineer who didn't last a week out on the rig because he couldn't handle the heat! Another time, a friend looked with envy at my lifestyle and wanted it too. Thinking it would be like being on extended holiday, she persuaded her partner to take an overseas contract, sadly she didn't last more than three months, before she packed it in and headed home, leaving her partner behind to complete the contract. It's not a lifestyle for everyone. You need resilience, adaptability and you need to deliver the goods.

Where to Begin?

The best way to start is by asking yourself the values questions, (see Chapter 9) as they will quickly show you what you most highly value and what is most important to you. Be honest and see how many times three or four words keep reappearing in your answers. Use a highlighter to colour code the answers. Or keep a tally until a pattern becomes clear.

> *"Knowing yourself is the start of living a fulfilled and satisfying life."*

When I did this process for myself I came up with travel, research, writing and teaching, but only after three attempts. Then the question I asked, was this,

> *"If travel is my highest value, how can I be paid to travel?"*

This is how this book came about. I realised I had been paid to travel for more than twenty-five years and now I just needed a new way to do it! I went in search of a new and better way.

What are your highest values? It may or may not be travel. Whatever it is, if you discover what you value most, and pursue that with **passion, presence, perseverance, participation and performance,** you have the greatest chance of making a success of your life.

This self-inquiry will give you the clues you need to follow your dreams.

At the end of each chapter in the book you will discover the **key takeaways** from each of the experts interviewed. In the final chapter you will discover how to uncover these keys for yourself, you will have a comprehensive explanation of the Values Test, what questions you need to ask yourself, and how to connect the dots and answer the question:

How Can I Be Paid to Travel?

For more information and FREE resources to go www.merrianstyles.com

CHAPTER TWO

Confidence on Camera

Natasha Zuvela

MTV Presenter

"You don't have to be great to get started.
You just have to get started to be great."

Les Brown

CHAPTER TWO

Confidence on Camera

Natasha Zuvela

MTV Presenter

Many of you might be among the 5000 viewers watching Natasha on your TV screens when she presented with Steve Irwin on *Wildlife Warrior* shows, or you may have seen her as the face of Curves Women's Fitness in Australia and New Zealand. As a TV presenter with over 60 million viewers, she's a familiar face in many households around the globe. These days, Natasha is often flying around the world working with industry leaders and Fortune 500 companies and their CEOs, as well as presenting her program 'Confidence on Camera'. Welcome Natasha.

Natasha: Thank you, Merrian. I've been really looking forward to having a chat with you today. And yes, it's going to be a good conversation, so thank you for having me.

Merrian: I'd like to start our talk with just getting a little background. Where did you start your journey? Did you just wake up one morning and decide when you were seven that you wanted to be a TV presenter?

Natasha: No. When I was five, actually, I was very shy and nervous. I wouldn't actually get off my mum's leg. I went everywhere she went hiding behind her, groping her calf. For my mother, it was like, "I just need to get Natasha off my leg and get her a little bit more confident". I was so nervous and shy. My mother decided to enrol me in modelling classes as a five-year-old to really build my confidence. The journey started there, where I began to enjoy being in front of an audience and to love and get comfortable with an audience at that young age, purely to gain confidence.

That's really where the journey started. I didn't really have in mind that I wanted to be a TV presenter. It just evolved as the years went by, especially learning about grooming, deportment, and I really started to fall in love with doing photography and getting photographed as a model. It kind of evolved many years down the track through my sporting career as well.

> *"I have three loves, that's entertainment, sports, and personal empowerment."*

As a teenager, I became a two times Australian Aerobics Champion. I was very into health and fitness as a young teenager, and I really learned discipline, focus and direction from a very young age. Being a sportsperson and loving the entertainment world, as well as modelling, I really felt that the next step for me was to embrace what I loved which was acting and television presenting. I didn't set out to become an actor or think I'd like being in the media industry. It just evolved naturally.

Merrian: Am I right in thinking you were a teacher of gymnastics as well as aerobics?

Natasha: No, I was actually the least flexible person in high school, but I have a very strong determination. Actually, when I put my mind to something, even if I'm not very good at it, I want to master it and get really good at it, and that's always been my philosophy. With aerobics, I had a certain level of muscular, physical attributes to move into that sport, but flexibility didn't come naturally. I really had to work hard at that. I spent hours and hours training before and after school. I think I was training up to 20 hours a week as a teenager, plus doing school and playing for multiple different basketball teams at different levels. I really learned and **mastered discipline, focus and direction** from an early age, and it kind of evolved from there into other areas of my career.

Challenges

Merrian: Right. I was going to ask you what your greatest challenges were, but you've just listed them for me. One of them was confidence, one of them was mastering determination and setting goals and achieving those goals and actually sticking with something. Are there any other challenges that you would like to share with us?

Natasha: Sure, those were challenges, as a teenager and especially in my early part of my childhood, my childhood wasn't the greatest in many ways, I experienced abuse as a child when I was quite young, and as much as I'd like to think that I got over that, I actually didn't really… It took me many, many years of dealing with that, and that's where I found the love of personal development. Not knowing I had that experience and trying to not really remember those experiences as a child, I would escape through choosing not the best boyfriends for me, the group of people that I ended up hanging out with were not the best choices. I struggled with **depression** for many years, **drugs**, really, really **low self-worth** for many years and I actually covered up that for quite some time.

That was probably one of my biggest challenges to overcome, feeling self-worth again, feeling that I was worth more than my past experiences, and actually believing that I could have a great life, a great relationship. I could have amazing friends, and I could actually start to have a life that I loved. And being in the media industry, you don't really talk about that stuff. It's a presentation. You don't express all those things.

> *"One of my greatest challenges was learning to believe that I was actually worth more than my past."*

And when I really understood that, that's when things really started to change for me, and that's where the love of personal development came in. It's from my own journey, knowing that I could overcome those challenges and help other people do the same.

Merrian: I love that. And so many of us struggle with self-worth and finding the keys to overcome those challenges can be a lifelong search without the right help.

Natasha: Absolutely. Even knowing what I've been through and what I've achieved, as a mum with two kids under four, running a business, travelling, and then maintaining a healthy relationship is an absolute challenge at times. There's just new challenges, just on different levels, so it's a constant adjustment and being flexible and **being open to change** is probably the biggest thing that's enabled me to achieve the things that I have achieved in my life, but I tell you it's a constant juggle.

"Progress is more important than perfection."

And some days are better than others. And the days that are challenging, I just have to stop and go, "Hang on a second". I looked where I was ten years ago, I wasn't in a very good place, look where I am today, it's literally worlds apart. You've just got to remind yourself that no matter what you go through, you can get through anything. It's knowing that you've come from a worse place than you are at now, and just embrace that.

Merrian: Yes. I hear what you're saying because I know that sometimes, when you get presented with a similar challenge again, and you think, "Gosh! I thought I've been here and done with this, why is this coming up for me again?" And you sometimes step up and go, "Well, maybe it's not that I haven't learned that lesson. Perhaps, it's that I can now acknowledge it in my conscious awareness and appreciate how far I've come."

Natasha: Yes, and that's it. And there's great quote:

And for someone who works in the media industry, there's a lot of perfection, but it's not about being perfect, it's about moving forward and knowing that as long as you move, even if it's a half a step, that's okay. It's the progress that's more important than actually going, "Oh, I've got to get it all perfect." So yes, I agree with you.

Merrian: As women, we often want it all to be perfect before we even begin. That's a great lesson for us all to learn that we just have to start, and if mistakes happen, it's okay, because we can always do better. But the aim is always, "I'm just doing my best."

Natasha: Absolutely. There's a great quote from Les Brown,

> *"You don't have to be great to get started.*
> *You just have to get started to be great."*

And I think life would have been easier, if I had known this, especially at the beginning of my TV career, when I couldn't read out loud to save my life. I struggled with **dyslexia** in high school, and I would get humiliated about how I'd actually speak in public, never would I have thought I'd become an international TV presenter and a public speaker for a living.

It's not about being perfect and getting it right straight off the bat, it's just giving it a go. And I'm glad that I've given things a go even if I wasn't very good at them, but I just developed that skill that I'm just going to get better at it. And if I keep working at it, I will get there. I will master the skills. That's really important to keep in mind when you're starting any new venture, or getting into any new relationship or going in business or whatever it is, you've just got to get started, no matter what your skill level is.

Just Start

Merrian: Perfect, I love that. You've obviously had people you've worked with mentor you, who inspire you, could you tell us a little bit about who they are, why that has worked for you?

Natasha: Yes, I've had amazing people in my life, people I like to call guardian angels, in a spiritual sense, looking out for me but I've had some amazing coaches, especially the pivotal moment in my lowest point in my life, well over ten years ago now. I had a wonderful coach named Rose who I met in Perth, because that's where I was born and bred, in Western Australia. Rose was absolutely pivotal in my transition in rebuilding my life again, and I am forever grateful to this lady. It was my commitment to change, but also her commitment to me to just support me in that process, I truly am grateful to that woman. I would literally say she did save my life through a tough period.

I've also had amazing coaches and actors who helped me progress my TV career, the late, great Billy Brown who was my very first voice coach. When I first started in MTV, I was terrible and the ratings were not going well, so my director said:

> *"We really need you to lift your game when you're presenting on camera."*

He was my first coach in the media industry, and he helped me transform the way I presented on camera and really helped get that engagement through my voice. He was amazing as a coach and mentor. Now I have amazing mentors, I like Ali Brown in the US, who's just phenomenal as a female entrepreneur and the way she coaches and guides me, which is just great. And there's many, many other ones, but I just would be here forever if I listed them all. They've really made a huge impact my life.

Take Action

The most important thing is that I've actually **taken action** and implemented what my mentors have suggested. They've given me guidance, but I've actually done something with it and gone for it, I suppose is the word, but having their guidance definitely has assisted to create the success that I have today.

Merrian: And you've also asked for help, many women just don't ask for help. We just think that we can do it all, and we can do it alone, and we struggle until we crumble. And then when we're in a puddle at the bottom. We kind of go, "Well, maybe getting some help would be a good idea." Asking for help is also another thing that many of us struggle with, and so kudos to you. You've gone out there and sought some help and got some help, but even more importantly, you've taken the action and done what they've been asking you to do. That's a very courageous thing to do.

Natasha: Thank you. There comes a point where, in any woman's life, if things aren't working, there's got to be another way. You've just got to **find another way**. As much as we think we can do it all, it's a pipe dream to be able to do everything. I know a lot of women don't ask, and they're in different positions, but if you can get support even from a friend or something that doesn't have to cost money, or change your environment, try and find people that are in **alignment with your thinking and your values** and just find people that can support you and not tell you that you have to pay to get coached, but find people that have similar interests and values to you that can help guide you, if you are going through a tough time – getting support is not weakness, it's actually strength.

I've had to learn that myself, especially now with two kids under four and running a business. Having help, just to help me keep sane because it's just near impossible to run the business that I'm running without having support with the kids. Sometimes I feel like, "Oh, I need to do it all," but I'm like, "Well, and who is that serving? My kids, myself, or my business?" It's not serving anyone, trying to be everything to everyone.

Merrian: I'm hearing you. I hear many businesswomen saying what they need is a wife.

Natasha: A wife, that's right.

Merrian: Taking care of everything else while we take care of the business.

Stay Present

Natasha: And I think one of the biggest things for women is actually having the family life, having the business, and making sure that you are present in those areas at that time. If you're working in the business, be present in the business. If you're with the kids, don't think about the business or work on other things that are going on, just stay present and focused on the kids. One of my biggest challenges is to separate those two and make sure that I'm **present and connected and focused** on each of those – the business and then making sure that I'm focused on the kids when I am with the kids. And that's one of the biggest challenges, especially working from home.

Merrian: What you are describing, it's actually being in the NOW, you're actually putting yourself in the NOW and dealing with what's in front of you right now and giving attention to that right now, which is... It's actually a skill that you need to acquire. I found that I needed to acquire, and one of the ways that I did it was through meditation. Do you have any tips on how you keep yourself centred and focused?

Natasha: Yes. One of my biggest keys to the success that I've had and also just to stay, to keep things rolling in family, in business, and travel, is to really, and I know this sounds cliché, but is to really be thankful for what I have right now. Not focusing on, "Oh, I wish this could be better, I wish I had more time, or I wish I had more wealth." It's to really be grateful for everything that I have right now in my life. That helps me stay centred. It helps me stay positive.

Be Grateful

Some days are harder than others, but that is one of the keys that brings me back to centre and helps me stay present with the kids and present in the business is to be grateful for what I have, because I've come a long way from where I used to be. And I'm just going to remind myself that I'm not there, I'm here, and be grateful for that. But that would be one of my keys to the success that I've had.

Merrian: That's beautiful. Are there downsides to success?

Natasha: Downsides? Yes, there are. I've put in a lot of effort and time and long hours. There's lack of sleep. That's probably to do with my two kids still waking up through the night.

Merrian: That's motherhood.

Natasha: Yes, that's motherhood. But I would say the amount of time I've invested, the money that I've invested in my career, in the training courses, the effort, you put a lot into it. I could be relaxing more on the weekends or maybe going to bed earlier, or enjoying more relaxation time, that would be the downside. You don't have as much time to relax.

You really have got to be conscious of making time. I think time and the financial investment that I've spent on myself, and in the business, but I'm reaping the rewards now.

At the time, you have got to almost have a **leap of faith** and go yes, you just go invest in yourself and know that it will work out. You've got to have that belief first or otherwise, you'll kind of go, "I can't spend this money on myself, or I shouldn't be spending it on this program or this course." It comes back to the self-belief in whether you think you can really do it.

Merrian: And if you're worth it.

Natasha: And if you're worth it.

Merrian: Because it's investment in yourself, isn't it?

Natasha: Yes.

Merrian: So, you had a leap of faith, and took action. That leads me to asking, what do you consider to be the benefits of taking that leap of faith, out of your comfort zone and into the unknown?

Rewards and Benefits

Natasha: The key benefit is that the reward and the treasure on the other side of that fear or that leap of faith is far greater than staying in that safety net, or staying in that comfort zone. For me, it's like overcoming my phobia of snakes for 25 years to become a certified venomous snake handler.

Merrian: Oh, my gosh. What's that like?

Natasha: That's right. Look, had I not faced that fear, I would never have had the opportunity to be part of Steve Irwin's dream, take over part of his role as the main crocodile host at Australia Zoo, and I would never have gotten appreciation for how amazing animals are, particularly snakes. I never thought I would ever say that in my entire my life.

I was really stretched out of my comfort zone, but what that did for me psychologically and mentally was enabled me to push further and go, **"Well, if I can do that, what else can I do?"** That freedom of knowing now when I walk through a bush, I'm looking for snakes instead of freaking out going, "Oh, my gosh! I hope that I don't cross a snake." And now, I can go for a walk and not be concerned about whether a snake is going to cross my path because I can probably pick it up and move it to another place.

Merrian: What an amazing accomplishment.

Overcoming Fears

Natasha: Yes. Overcoming your fears, taking that leap of faith, what it does for you and what it did for me personally was enabled me to trust myself and know that there is so many more amazing things to do when you **step out of your comfort zone**. Really, the treasure is on the other side of those doorways of fear in your life, there are far more rewards than there are downsides. It gives you much more confidence in yourself and more self-belief.

Merrian: Brilliant. What would you think would be your three biggest mistakes, or three biggest regrets? Often people say, when you've made a mistake, there are actually no mistakes, there are just learning opportunities. What might you have learned from those that you've actually taken in, integrated and gone, "Okay, didn't do that quite so well, but now, I've moved on and I actually know what that flaw is or what that issue is. I can actually absorb that and move on and actually turn it into a positive."

No Mistakes, Only Opportunities

Natasha: I agree, there are no mistakes. I totally agree with that because they're all leading you to the path where you are meant to be. And unless you have those experiences, you just don't fully appreciate it when you do you get to a certain stage in your life and you go:

> *"Wow, had I not experienced that, I wouldn't have valued what I have today."*

Relationships being one of them, I wasn't very good at relationships. I just didn't believe that I was worth more and I would attract relationships that did not serve me, and no fault to the person that I was dating, but it just wasn't conducive to my health, and I didn't believe that I could actually have an amazing man in my life.

One of my biggest mistakes was not believing, at that time, that I was worth more, I had numerous relationship that were not healthy and until I actually stopped and did the work and believed that I was worth more, then I actually attracted the man that I have today. I spent years and years and years searching for that person, at the time, I never thought I was worth more than what I was getting. I would say if I would have had a lot more belief in myself early in my life, then I would not have experienced the challenges that I did, then I wouldn't be able to serve and help people now in the form that I do, with my *Courage to Shine* book and program.

Merrian: I'd love to come back and have another interview with you about that whole relationship question, because that's a really big one, and I really hear what you're saying because I know, from my own experience, that I attracted unavailable men for many years. And until I stepped back and went, "What am I doing, and what is it that is in me that I need to look at to overcome in order to attract the right kind of man?" That's a whole other topic.

Natasha: Yes, the whole relationship thing… I've had some interesting ones.

Merrian: I look forward to comparing notes with you on relationships. Is there a question that I haven't asked you that you would like me to ask you?

Natasha: Well, I think we're good.

Merrian: How about where to next?

Where to Next?

Natasha: Oh, where to next? That's always a good question. Where to next for me is I'm about to launch my book, *Courage to Shine* which is a revamp of my original book, *The Crocodile Effect*. I'm relaunching that with the help of Fiona Jones, who's just tying things up for the book, so that's really exciting. I have an online program that goes with that book, the *Courage to Shine*. Rebranding and relaunching the Natasha Zuvela brand, and we have "Shine on Camera," but I'm really now putting the focus on the **"Video Brand Power""** and **Natasha Zuvela brand** and moving more into the **female empowerment** space, which is really exciting.

It's why I got into business. It's where my heart is, empowering women specifically, but also men and really helping them really have the courage to shine and not hold back and not worry what about other people think, and really share their story and their journey without

worrying about being criticised or judged, and just being themselves. That's exciting for me because it's something that I've wanted to do for a little while now, but my attention has been on my kids and building the "Shine on Camera" business, and also launching some new episodes in my YouTube channel, which is in the next two to three months will be evolving as well.

Exciting things ahead.

Merrian: That sounds very exciting. Where will people find more about you, your programs, which website address would you like them to be directed to? Would you like to share some of those contacts?

Natasha: My "Courage to Shine" website, or my "Courage to Shine" programs are based under the **NatashaZuvela.com** website, all around my *Courage to Shine* book; and now personal empowerment programs are under that website. If you're looking for more on camera training and learning how to be a real influencer online using powerful engaging video, then you'll head to the ShineOnCamera.com.au website. It all depends on where you're at and what you need.

Most of it right now, whether it's to learn how to be more engaging on camera, then Shine on Camera's the website for you, or if you're looking for more empowerment and getting more confidence and motivation to really step up and try and shine brightly, then NatashaZuvela.com would be the best website to go to.

Merrian: Natasha, thank you so much for all your valuable insights.

Natasha: I enjoyed the chat. I'm sure we'll be chatting more about relationship.

Merrian: I'm sure we will, and it's been such a pleasure spending time with you, and I look forward to our next discussion about relationships. Thank you so much.

Natasha: Thanks, Merrian.

Key Takeaways:

- Overcome your limitations. Whether its lack of confidence, lack of self-worth, lack of skills, limiting beliefs, identify what is holding you back and take steps to overcome your limitations.
- Be flexible, open and committed to change.
- Be grateful for all you have in your life and more will flow to you.
- You don't have to be perfect you just have to start. Take Action.
- Align your thinking with your values.
- Get out of your comfort zone and give it a go. Take that leap of faith.
- Stay present and focused. If something is not working find another way.
- There are no mistakes or failures, only opportunities to do better.
- Invest in yourself, invest in self-development, a mentor whatever you need to make it happen.
- In times of doubt, look back and see how far you've come and keep going!

CHAPTER THREE

The World is My Home

Dr John Demartini

Transformational Speaker and Author

"The universe is my playground, the world is my home. Every country is a room in the house and every city is a platform I can share my heart and soul."

Dr John Demartini

CHAPTER THREE

The World is My Home

Dr John Demartini
Transformational Speaker and Author

Dr John Demartini is an international bestselling author, a human behavior specialist and a renowned public speaker. He was also featured in the movie and book, *The Secret* and his signature event is "The Breakthrough Experience." He's also written *The Values Factor* which was instrumental in my own personal development and growth. Welcome, Dr Demartini.

Merrian: When you set out on your travels at an early age, you were bumming around Hawaii as a backpacker and you had an epiphany. Can you tell us about that and how it changed your life?

John: I was a high school dropout, I was a street kid and I picked up surfing in Texas. You need to have hurricanes to have good surf there. I left my home at 13, and I hitchhiked to California when I was 14. I panhandled and bummed money and did all sorts of odd jobs and whatever I could to survive. I wanted to surf the North Shore, so I went out there and I first slept under the Kamehameha Highway Bridge at Sunset Beach.

Then I social-climbed and went into Ehukai Beach Park and slept under a park bench. And from there, when it rained, I went into the bathrooms because they had a shelter. And from there I found an abandoned car, and slowly I social-climbed into a tent and grass house combination in the jungle. I surfed every day, up to 11 hours a day. I'd go out surfing three and sometimes four times a day. I was eating whatever was available, I would eat pineapples and avocados and mangoes were plentiful. I found bananas and avocados wherever they were and ate coconuts. And literally I lived on about $2 a day.

Life Changing Moment

I wasn't taking care of my health, and I was eating a particular plant there that had toxic material in it without realizing it and I ended up with strychnine, cyanide poisoning. At first, I started cramping my fingers and toes. And everybody said John, you're surfing 11 hours a day. You must have electrolyte imbalances. I tried to take potassium to compensate for that, nothing helped and it kept getting worse. It started going from toes and fingers up into my wrist, and then into my ankles and up to my elbows. I didn't know what it was.

Eventually it stopped my diaphragm from working and I almost died.

To make a longer story short, I ended up passing out in front of a parking lot of a supermarket. And somehow, somebody recognised me and I guess knew where my tent was and took me to my tent, because three and half days later I woke up in my tent. I had been pretty cathartic and sick, those three and a half days. Luckily a lady found me and helped me recover. She led me to a health food store to try to regain some strength, and one day leaving the health food store, I saw a little flyer on the door.

Something intuitively said, go to this talk.

I never went to talks, I wasn't interested in anything like that at the time. I was told in first grade I would never be able to read or write or communicate, never amount to anything, not go very far in life. I was a high school dropout. I had never even read a book in my life. I had learning problems, speech problems, all kinds of things. But I intuitively went to this talk. It was at the sunset recreational hall and there was a yogi woman there, who introduced a gentleman named Paul Bragg.

> *"In one hour that one man with his one message that one night was speaking to me he changed my life."*

After hearing him speak, he was so inspiring and so present and so purposeful that all I could say is that was the first night in my entire life that I thought, maybe I could overcome my learning problems and maybe someday I could be intelligent. I just assumed I was never going to be an academic. That night, after meeting with Paul Bragg I had a dream that I could be intelligent. I thought a teacher was intelligent. I thought, I'd love to be a teacher. I'd love to learn, I'd love to conquer my reading problems and speech problems.

And that night my life changed.

A New Beginning

That was the beginning of a new trajectory of my life and I started meditating like he told me, and I started talking to myself differently. I started listening to him, I tried to pick up a book. The first book I ever picked up was *Chico's Organic Gardening and Natural Living*, which is a book on gardens. It had a long-haired hippy guy on the front cover and I thought, if that guy could write, then I could read it. I started my journey of trying to overcome my learning problems. **I started meditating every day**, and one day in the meditation, a little voice in my head said it's time to go and see your parents, you haven't seen them in years.

And I flew back to LA, hitchhiked back to Texas. And my mom was waiting for me, and she didn't know I was coming home, but she was there in the kitchen and said, "Oh my God!" She didn't recognise me, because I had long hair and a beard. And she said, "Welcome home." Two days later, my mom and dad encouraged me to take a GED, a high school equivalency test, because I had nothing to lose by trying the test. If I passed, I had a high school diploma to try to get jobs. I guessed and passed, miraculously. And Paul Bragg, the teacher that inspired me, said every single day to overcome your learning problems. Say:

"I'm a genius and I apply my wisdom."

I have said that every single day, I've never missed a day in 43-plus years. I say it every day because:

"I now believe that a genius is one who listens to the inner voice and inner vision, follows the inner vision of their soul and obeys."

And I passed that test, my parents encouraged me to take a college entrance exam, in case I ever wanted to go to college somewhere. And I took that and I guessed and I passed, literally guessed and passed.

The Lows

Then I took my first college class and I thought I was going to do well like the other tests and I bombed it, I got a 27. Everybody else had 75 to 100. I was really discouraged. I ran to my car, I cried in my car. I couldn't believe it, I just felt so humiliated. All I could hear is my first grade teacher saying I'll never read, I'll never write, I'll never communicate, never amount to anything, or go very far in life.

And I drove home crying and I curled up in a foetal position in the living room at my parent's house under this bible stand, which stands in my office today. When my mom died, I got that. It's very special to me. And I just sat there and had a low moment and thought, this whole thing was a delusion about being a teacher and being intelligent. And my mom came home from shopping and she saw me there, and she said, "Son, what happened?" I said, "I've bombed the test. I blew it. I guess I'll never read, I'll never write, I'll never communicate and all that stuff."

My mom knew what to say, in fact she put her hand on my shoulder and she said, "Son, whether you become a great teacher, healer and philosopher, travel the world like you dream, whether you ride big waves, giant waves like you've done in Hawaii, whether you return to the street and panhandle as a bum, I just want to let you know, that your dad and I are going to love you no matter what."

Their expectation on me was an **unconditional love**, particularly my mom. They didn't know if I was ever going to finish school. So anything I would do in that direction, they thought was special. When she said that, my hand went into a fist and I looked up and I saw a vision of me speaking in front of a million people and all from a balcony, looking out at a giant square, and which is a painted by Andrew Tischler, a famous painter, and it sits in my office as a vision.

Becoming a Master

I said to myself, I'm going to master these things called reading and learning and studying. I'm going to master this thing called teaching and travelling and:

> *"I'm going to do whatever it takes, travel whatever distance and pay whatever price to give my service of love across the planet. And I'm not going to let any human being stop me from it, not even myself."*

Then I hugged my mom. I went to my room and I got a dictionary and I started memorizing a dictionary, 30 words a day. With the help of my mom, my vocabulary grew 30 words a day. I had to spell to it, pronounce it properly, add meaning to it, put it in a sentence, and slowly but surely my vocabulary got strong enough to pass school.

I was relentless from that day on in reading, and I started reading encyclopaedias. I read eight complete sets of encyclopaedias, and I started devouring books. About a year later my mom asked me what I wanted for my birthday, because my birthday was on Thanksgiving day. I said,

> *"Mom, I want the greatest teachings and greatest writings from around the world by the greatest thinkers, and the greatest minds."*

And she said, "Sure you don't want a t-shirt?" I said, "No mom, I just want the greatest writings on earth. I want to learn. I want to learn the laws of the universe." So she contacted her brother, who was a professor at MIT, my uncle.

The Gift

As a gift, a very special gift, he sent two giant six-by-six-by-six foot wooden crates on a flatbed truck down to our home. They took them off the flat bed and onto the ground, and I took a crowbar and opened it all up, and brought in thousands of books, literally thousands of books, into my room and just filled it up, just literally put this massive library into my room. I had a yoga mat in the centre and I just sat and I read 20 hours a day until I started excelling.

Slowly but surely, as I was starting to excel and started to do well in school and eventually I was the top student, people kept asking me questions and I started teaching. My first student was a 375-pound Afro-American woman, who wanted me to teach her yoga, which is impossible. Next a gentleman asked me to teach him meditation. Then 16 or 17 people came in and asked me to teach them mathematics.

When I left the Wharton, I went on to University of Houston, and every day, pretty well under the trees or in the cafeteria, I had 100 to 150 students gathered. And I was teaching by then, and I was learning how to speed-read and develop reading capacities. I was reading about a book an hour or 45 minutes to an hour. I started getting up to very high speeds. And I just kept doing it.

When I went onto professional school, I kept teaching six, seven nights a week. It just kept spreading into the community and then finally the city, and then the state, and then finally, nationally. I think I spoke in all the 52 states in America and then around the world. I started in Canada then I went to Europe. Now we have students in every country on earth. If you stay with something long enough, you get somewhere.

Love of Travel

Merrian: On that note, one of your goals was to set foot in every country in the world. Travel is one of your highest values. Why is travel important to you?

John: When I was born, my foot was turned and my arm was turned in. I had to wear braces till age of four, and I had to go to speech pathologist for speech impediment. When I turned four, I begged my dad, I said:

> *"Please let me out of these things, I promise to keep my arm and legs straight."*

"It's swell if you do, then great. If you don't, I got to put you back in the braces." From that day on, the second I got out of them, because I'd been constrained and people kind of make fun of you when you're wearing braces all the time, you want to run and you want to be free. I think that had an impact on me, I'm assuming, looking back at least rationally that makes sense.

By the time I was four, I was, believe it or not, I was small enough to go down in the sewers and I was running through the sewers in the city, just exploring the sewers. I was running down the streets. When I was nine, I had my first little company, a little landscaping company. I bought my own bicycle. My dad made me accountable, he made me pay for room, clothing and rent because he wanted me to be a little entrepreneur, because I wasn't academically inclined. He said I could ride my bicycles in any directions, as long I was home at nine o'clock.

I started riding my bicycle 35 miles. Then by age 12, I was hopping trains from city to city. By age 13, I was hitchhiking from city to city. By 14, I had hitchhiked across America to California and throughout Mexico. I snuck in to Mexico illegally, got out of there illegally. I was amazed, I got in and out of there.

I've been a traveller all my life, and I felt at home travelling. Right now, I'm in New Zealand. I'm in Auckland. I just came in from Sydney, Brisbane actually. I'm a full-time traveller, I've done 17,000,000 miles in flights now.

Citizen of the World

When I was 18 years old and my uncle sent books to me, one of the books was on Albert Einstein, another one was on a great philosopher, Epictetus. And Epictetus said that when he was writing about Socrates:

> *"Socrates said 'I'm not a man of Corinth, I'm not a man of Athens. I'm a citizen of the universe'."*

Albert Einstein when they asked him about his family life he said,

> *"I'm not really a man of my family. I'm not a man of my community or city, or even state or nation. I'm a citizen of the world and the universe."*

I always felt that that resonated with me. So I've said since I was 21:

> *"The universe is my playground, the world is my home. Every country is a room in the house and every city is a platform I can share my heart and soul."*

After 9/11 – my wife and I were living in Trump Tower at the time, when 9/11 hit – they weren't letting people in the tower because they thought the tower was going to go down next. Athena ended up flying over to another one of our homes in Australia. I was not scheduled to be in Australia, until later that year, I said, I'm not going to see you unless we come up with Plan B.

Two years earlier I saw the advertisement for the ship, *The World*, but I wasn't quite ready to buy then, because it only had 27% occupancy, I thought it was a little risky. But then I had dinner with somebody that actually bought on *The World* and investigated it. The next day, as an anniversary gift, I bought a condominium on the ship *The World* and I've lived there for the past fifteen years.

The ship was perfect. On the day of the launch in Norway, at this special amazing function with just the residents only, the captain said, "Welcome to your new home, *The World*. Every country is a room in the house." It was identical to what I had been saying since 21. I got tears in my eyes, I thought:

Destiny

"Wow! It's amazing what you say to yourself, how it impacts your destiny."

Merrian: Absolutely. One of your other sayings is, "Get on the way and not in the way." What do you mean by that?

John: The actual statement is:

"A master sees things on the way not in the way,"

which means that they learn to ask questions because the quality of your life is based on the quality of the questions you ask.

Ask yourself:

Q How specifically is whatever I'm experiencing today, whether supportive or challenging, how is it helping me fulfil my highest values?

Q What is most meaningful?

Q What is my mission?

Q What am I dedicated to?

Don't stop answering that until you have enough answers or you have a tear of gratitude for what's happening. And then you realise nothing is in your way. It's all about perception.

William James, father of modern psychology, around 1895 or so, said:

"The greatest discovery of his generation was that human beings can alter their life by altering their perceptions and attitude of mind."

By asking new questions, it changes perceptions and attitudes, and you see things on the way.

Challenges

Merrian: Your teaching is much about balance, and wherever there is a challenge, there is a benefit, what have been your greatest adult challenges?

John: I had challenges when I was married to my first wife. I had challenges trying to fit into a normal routine, kind of a go to work, come home, live in a suburban house. I attempted to live that lifestyle, but in my heart I just couldn't. When I was 20, I had a mentor named Ed Tollison. Ed said something to me that was really inspiring to me. He said:

> *"Never live where you can't see the furthest horizons. Never let anybody else's construction interfere with your vision."*

I always want to live in high rises on the top floor, penthouses or I want to live on top of the mountain. Or I want to be in the sky on a private jet, or I want to be at sea, where there is nothing blocking my view.

I tried to live in a suburban place, with a fence and a house with my wife, because that was her need. She was grounding me and I was not ready to be grounded at the time. I struggled with that because really, I wanted to travel the world and I felt claustrophobic living in one place, and trying to be somebody that wasn't me.

That's why I guess I'm so adamant about helping people find what they really value and be authentic to themselves because I was living by my parents' expectation, social expectations. Kohlberg said that most people are subordinate to mothers, fathers, preachers, teachers or peer pressure from community, city, state, nation or world. And few people make it to transcendence, where they're actually giving themselves permission to set the rules and create a complete new paradigm for life, and set their own pathway.

> *"Losing yourself in travel serves to uncover that moment when you realise you have everything you are searching for, then your travels transform into a journey of self-discovery..."*
>
> **Merrian Styles**

I felt inside there was a yearning, but I was trying to fit in. I finally had to break through that. We parted and she deserved to have what she wanted,

I deserved to have what I wanted. And today, I see the perfection of how she was in my life, she was actually the perfect person because she gave me three beautiful children.

One of my children is doing what I'm doing and helping me today. One has got a fashion company, Demartini Fashion. My son is emerging and he's helping out in our adventures, and it's not quite sure exactly what he's going to do, but he's definitely on track. But if I wouldn't have had my wife in my life, I wouldn't have those children and those children are very special. There was no mistake, but we both had our own destinies and we had to go our own paths.

I'm very grateful for that, but at the same time, I did feel claustrophobic. That was a challenge. I wasn't intending to get divorced. I just knew I couldn't live that way anymore. We had two different ideas about what we wanted to do.

Delegate

Then I had other challenges. I've had many challenges with schedules, because I keep a very intense schedule. I do a thousand interviews on average a year now, and I write for about 50 or 70 magazines a month. Then I'm also speaking, I'm right at 150 speeches so far this year I'm on track for about 340. With that schedule, plus consulting and all these other things, I keep a very busy schedule.

And I attempt to do all the other things I'm doing with family and relationship and everything else. Trying to keep all that going and hoping that flights are on time, and hotels are, if I'm delayed, they don't give away my rooms and things like that. Those are my challenges.

I've delegated most everything in my life, all I do is research, write, travel and teach. I don't do much anything else. I don't cook. I don't drive. I haven't driven in 26 years, I haven't cooked in 35 years. I don't do anything other than research, write, travel and teach. I've simplified most things, but occasionally I'll get into challenges with flights or hotels.

That's about it, that's about my biggest challenge now, and meeting deadlines. Trying to get books written or articles done. Sometimes I'm up until three in the morning, getting those done. Crazy schedules.

Merrian: Because you love it, it's not work?

John: No, it's not work. It's just that sometimes, because I'm in a different country, sometimes there will be different time-zones and different time expectations that are in different countries. Yesterday I sent off to Japan a manual that they need to print and translate, they need three months to translate this thousand-page manual. I had to send that off and I had a deadline, and I wanted to make sure I got that out.

Today for example, I got up at ten past three this morning to get a flight, and I needed to get that manual finished. I got that finished at two in the morning. I just meditate. I showered and meditated for an hour and here I am. Those are my challenges. Also, occasionally I get people who are challenging to deal with. You know clients that are challenging or attendees that are challenging or promoters that are challenging, but nothing that's extraordinary.

Bigger Vision

Merrian: One of the things that you raise in your talks is having a bigger vision, something bigger than yourself. I know that you've established the Demartini Institute. Would you talk a little bit about what that bigger vision is for you, and how would you like to be remembered?

John: I have some really corny jokes sometimes and some of them are perverted, and I'm afraid that's what they'll remember me by.

Merrian: How would you choose to be remembered?

John: Jokes aside, they'll remember something important. In 1982, October 12, I was devouring the Vedic text. A teacher, guru, friend gave me 74 volumes of Vedic literature. I told him I'd have them summarised and condensed and written about everything else, and outlined in three months. I was working until the early hours of the morning, and it was about two in the morning on October 12.

I took a break from studying the text and I went and meditated because instead of sleeping I just found it more productive to meditate for an hour and then go back to work. In that meditation, I literally got a vision and heard a little inner voice that was really clear. And it said, "And they came, the world over." I wrote it down with tears in my eyes, and it was students from around the world.

Concourse of Wisdom

And then it said that you're to create a concourse of wisdom. The concourse of wisdom was a gathering of students from all countries, dedicated to love and wisdom. So I wrote that down. And then, I guess you'd call it automatic writing or something. I started writing outlines of 300 lessons from two-thirty in the morning till six-thirty I wrote it. I organised 300 classes, they just came pouring out of me, on every imaginable field that I had been studying, and I made a commitment to deliver those classes.

I got 27 of the brightest, well I actually contacted about 35 people, but 27 of the brightest people in Houston that I could find, physicists, artists, musicians, really genius people, leaders in business, I invite them to this little one-bedroom apartment, and I gave my first class.

> *"Balancing ego with humility is an evolutionary act."*
> **Merrian Styles**

And it was an exploration from the micro to the macro, from the subatomic world to the astronomical world. There was a meditation on imagining yourself living in a micro-world and a macro-world. It was a three-hour experience. Then I invited people back the next week to then study the mathematics of that journey, and three people showed up. I encouraged them to go to the third class and nobody showed up. I was a little disturbed because I was thinking, all the stuff I want to share, nobody is interested in it, apparently. It's too steep. I kind of had to postpone that until 1989. Then I got another vision on a flight going to Montreal to speak to a group of doctors in Quebec City.

The Breakthrough Experience

Then "The Breakthrough Experience" came. This was about 28 years ago. "The Breakthrough Experience" has been one of my signature programs for the last 28 years. I've taught that course 1,075 times. I've done it in 61 countries. That's been very key signature program. I'm going to do that here in New Zealand starting tomorrow.

I just started devouring anything to do with maximizing human awareness and potential in every field, 295 different disciplines. And try to integrate it towards one objective, how to maximise human beings. I want to have the most universal principles, which stand the test of time, to build a foundation of knowledge that people could stand on. That was the journey. But it started in a vision in 1982, October 12.

Merrian: The Demartini Institute teaches classes. What happens when you're no longer with us? What does the Demartini Institute do then?

John: What I'm working on right now is I'm taking the thousands of pages of writings I've done. It's a lot, 365,000 pages I think. I'm trying to put that into a series of collections of books. I'll put on as much of that as I can, probably in audio and video forms, slowly but surely. And then my daughter is going to carry on with the Demartini program, the training programs. She's carrying it on, she's doing an amazing job. She helped with Breakthrough program just the other day in Denver and from now on she'll be helping me.

Whether my son picks that up or not, I don't know. It's still early days for him. That's what's happening.

Then I have about 4000 facilitators that I have trained that disseminate my work around the world. One of them actually is in Israel, is a woman who has taught 2000 other ones there. We have 2000 Rabbis and their families that are using the method now. It's spreading.

You start with something and it just keeps growing. Little by little, there'll be people carrying on bits and pieces and their own versions. I'm sure that some will get deleted and some will get upgraded. But I'm just going to keep doing what I do and try to get as much down in writing and audio and video. Put online programs together and pass the torch to great students. Maybe your time has come and you're going to have to…

Merrian: Pass the torch to?

John: My daughter, I told her on my last week of my life that the only request I have from her is to have all the Victoria Secret models that have ever lived, there for me in the last week.

Merrian: Are they going to be the angels that take you over to the other side?

John: First make sure I'm going… I'm a student of angelology, I want to make sure I'm on the Angel side.

Merrian: I'm sure she'll make that happen for you.

John: Yeah, she will. She says, "Step aside, Gramps. I'm taking over. So you can warm with the angels."

Merrian: Dr Demartini, thank you very much for your time today.

John: Thank you. Appreciate the fun questions.

Merrian: Is there anything you'd like to add that I haven't asked you?

John: Yes I'd like to share with your readers, this statement that I found very meaningful.

"That no matter what I've done or not done, I'm worthy of love. And know that the only thing that nobody can take away from you is your love and wisdom. So give yourself permission to do something extraordinary on planet earth, and grow your love and wisdom for yourself and the world around you. And share that wisdom with people. It's rewarding, it's fulfilling and it's meaningful. You deserve to have an extraordinary life, and so give yourself permission to live an extraordinary life and do something extraordinary on planet earth." That's it.

Merrian: Wise words. Thank you very much.

John: Thank you, I appreciate the fun.

Key Takeaways:

- Establish your highest values and only do those.
- Delegate other tasks and focus on what is most important to you and you will succeed.
- Do what you love and it will not be work, it will be fulfilling your highest values.
- Persist and never give up.
- Listen to your inner voice and your intuition.
- Overcome your challenges and limitations.
- Reprogram your thoughts to support your dream.
- Give yourself permission to live an extraordinary life.
- Make time to meditate each day.
- Be grateful for all you have, the more grateful you are the more abundant your life will be.
- Know that the only thing that nobody can take away from you is your love and wisdom.
- No matter what you've done or not done, tell yourself you are worthy of love.

CHAPTER FOUR

Changing Habits, Changing Lives

Cyndi O'Meara

Nutritionist, Documentary Film Maker, Author and Speaker

"When crisis hits, opportunity comes to you".

Cyndi O'Meara

CHAPTER FOUR

Changing Habits, Changing Lives

Cyndi O'Meara

Nutritionist, Documentary Film Maker, Author and Speaker

Cyndi O'Meara is a nutritionist, bestselling author, international speaker, documentary creator, and founder of Changing Habits. Cyndi graduated with a bachelor of science from Deakin University in 1984 and has special interests for the ancestral foods. After completing her degree, she became so disillusioned with the nutritional guidelines that she paved her own path. And that was not without controversy. Her ground-breaking book, *Changing Habits, Changing Lives*, became an instant international bestseller. And from there, she has grown a successful organic food company, certified online education program, and created ground breaking documentary, *What's With Wheat?* I'd like to welcome you, Cyndi. Thank you for being with me today.

Cyndi: Thanks for having me.

Merrian: I'd like to start at the beginning, back in 1984. What were the reasons that you were disillusioned with the nutritional guidelines of the day? And what inspired you to pave a new pathway?

Cyndi: Well, it's interesting, because I was brought up in a very different household and a household that was very much into health, even back in the '60s and '70s. My mum was a nurse. My dad was a pharmacist, who saw where pharmacy was going in the '50s. And he just chose never to give us any medications while we were growing up. And I'm fortunate. I'm 56 years of age, and I've never had an antibiotic, Panadol, or aspirin, or any form of medication.

Merrian: Wow.

Cyndi: And it was because of his belief in the human body. Feed it the right food, stop interfering with it, and it can be the most healthy body possible. I knew I wanted to do something with health. I also wanted to ski and you can't do that in Australia. So I went to the University of Colorado in Boulder. And that's where my inspiration came. I had an amazing lecturer. His name was Dr Van Gerven. And he taught me anthropology and cultural anthropology and how food was important throughout our civilization from hunter-gatherer to agriculturist to herding society, industrial revolution. And I just got really intrigued by food and health.

Ancestral Health

I remember ringing my mum saying, "I'm leaving the University of Colorado. I want to come back. I want to be a dietician." That's when I went back to Deakin University, finished my degree. Didn't agree with anything that I was being taught, low-fat, manipulated foods, nothing to do with ancestral health, nothing. And I think that was where the disillusionment was because of the previous education I've had through my family and through the University of Colorado. And returning to Australia and not hearing the right things being taught, I became disillusioned.

I actually left the university after finishing my Bachelor of Science degree. I didn't go and become a dietician. I couldn't. I couldn't even imagine going to a hospital and then telling people to eat Jell-O and these amazing foods that they had come up with. And I looked at the foods, and I went, "I won't take that to anybody."

I went back to university for another two years, did human anatomy, pathology, histology, and embryology just to understand the human body better. I cut up cadavers for two years. And at the end of it, I went:

"You know what? It's not the dead ones I'm worried about. It's the live ones."

And what I learnt at the University of Colorado and what I know about the human body and everything that I've been doing, I went:

"I want to teach this type of nutrition."

And I put my shingle up, called myself a nutritionist, and taught ancestral health. Told people to go away from breakfast cereals and margarine and low fat and get back to their normal foods. And it was interesting back in the '80s, because a lot of people thought I was a little bit wacky saying go back to these original foods and stay away from these modern foods. But I think as time has gone on, we've realised that these modern foods have become a scourge of our health. And everybody seems to be teaching this now, this ancestral health.

First Mentor

I also had a mentor. I think mentors are really important, and he was Dr Bernard Jensen. I remember going to one of his conferences back in the mid-'80s, probably, when I'd just finished my degree and I was doing human anatomy. He just turned my head around. I realised that what I was saying was what he was saying. And he'd been saying it for a long time. He was lecturing when he was in his '80s and '90s. And he was a really good mentor. And now there are many more mentors out there that are saying the same thing.

Merrian: Brilliant. Gosh, cutting up cadavers for two years, that's very brave.

Cyndi: Yes, formaldehyde for two years.

Embracing Change

Merrian: Your book's called *Changing Habits, Changing Lives*. Generally speaking, people resist change. I'm one of the very few people that absolutely adore change, and I embrace it. But I know I'm the exception and not the rule. How do you initiate change in people's lives? How do you make changes in your life? And how do you actually motivate others to embrace change?

Cyndi: I think often it's a crisis that makes people change. More often than not, most people come to me in absolute crisis. They've tried every diet, or they've tried every modality for health. They are absolutely beside themselves. Those people change very quickly. Not all do, but usually those are the ones that change.

For those mothers out there that are saying that their children aren't as healthy as they'd like them to be, they know they've got to do better. They like to be educated. They want know:

> *"What do I do? How do I do it? What do I start with? How can I get the resources that you're talking about?"*

And that's what *Changing Habits, Changing Lives* is all about. It wasn't about a strict diet. It wasn't about this is how many calories you should have, how much fat you should have, how much carbohydrate. This was about teaching them about what they were eating and what our ancestors ate.

I would start with breakfast, I'd look at breakfast cereals… how are they made? What they are made of? What are the food fortifications? How was that food fortification made? Are you prepared to continue to eat this? You know, that was the question I would ask. I would go, "Now you know, well, are you going to continue to eat it?" because I think we blindly accept marketing and advertising to be truth. We blindly accept that anything that's on the grocery store is safe for us to eat. We accept that our government would never add something to our food that could possibly be a problem. But history tells us they have.

History Tells Us

History tells us from 500 years back that there were people adding sawdust to pepper, because pepper was expensive spice. They were adding bark and all sorts of things to pepper in order to just sell it at a reasonable price and make a lot of money. So we can't say that this hasn't been happening. History tells us. And in anything that I do, I always look back in history. I always look at what did we do, and why did we do it, and what are we doing now?

That's how the book happened – this is what they've done to our food. What's an alternative? I would never say, "Take that food out. You got nothing left." I would say, "Well, what's an alternative that we can use?" And I would do that with salt, with sugar, with chocolate, with milk, with dairy, with bread. So everything I talked about as to what they did to it… and I had educated myself about food additives, food preparation, food manufacturing. And by educating myself, I wanted to spread the word. And it started with my mothers' group.

How It Started

Here is how it all started… as a nutritionist, I'd done all this education. And then I started to have babies. And when you have babies, you don't seem to get out there and work as much as you used to do. But my mothers' group was really interested in why do you feed your kids that? Why do you not give your kids antibiotics? How do you keep your children off antibiotics? And why don't you give them Panadol when they've got a fever? I was asked all of these questions, and my mothers' group was very keen, and began seeing unbelievable change in my mothers' group. It was that that spurred me to go, "All right, well, what else can I do?" Why don't I start writing an article for the paper?" I wrote for the local paper. And it worked from there.

I think education is a big opener for change. But there are some people who don't want to be educated and will never change. I'm not even interested in even trying to change somebody who's not interested. And one of the things that I find is that if you put the information out there, and the people who are looking for that and are open to suggestion are the ones that will make those changes. In the beginning, I think, it's crisis. But for other people, it's education. So there are two modalities there. And I work on both.

The Challenges

Merrian: That's wonderful. I'm sure that in all of that, it didn't come easily and that you had experienced a challenge or two. What have been some of those challenges? And how did you overcome them?

Cyndi: I think one of the challenges was I was thinking outside the square. I wasn't thinking what everybody else was thinking. And so many people were criticizing what I had to say. They thought I was an idiot, a fool. I didn't know what I was talking about. And, you know, that's really hard when you're trying to pave the path that for them is a new path. For me, it was an old path. **To me, it was not revolutionary. It was evolutionary.** I could see where I was going. But for them, you know, they were looking down the barrel of a microscope and looking philosophically very differently. So, while their philosophies were challenged by my philosophies, I realised that they were just polarizing philosophies and that we would never see eye to eye. And so I had to let that go. I had to go:

"Well, I'm not going to convince everybody that this is the way to go."

But for those who were seeing this as common sense and that were following me, they're the ones that I want to concentrate on. And I have to tell you that the critic out there is usually the one that you see more than you see the people that are praising you or saying, "I like what you're saying. I'm improving." And if I was to, put that into two areas, 90% of the people that listen to what I'm saying are content and know that it's common sense, and realise it's the way they've got to go. It's very small percentages that are not seeing it that. I guess that's one of the challenges.

I think a second challenge was persistence. At times, I just wanted to give up. And I would give up… and I would go, "All right, that's it. I'm not doing it. I don't want to bother with this. You know, I'm quite happy doing what I'm doing. And why don't I just forget this?" But a day or two would pass, and I get bored. And I'd be going, "I can't do this. I might as well just keep going." And what I find happens is that if you know where you're going in life and what you want to do in your life and a challenge like that comes about, what then happens is that a new opportunity occurs.

Crisis and Opportunity

And so I'll give you an example. In my very young career… I think I was in my '30s. I'd just written my book *Changing Habits, Changing Lives*. So this was back in the '90s. And I spoke to about 150 people in my local town, in a group called… I think they were called Happy Slimmer's or something. And I was talking about why we should be eating real foods. And I'm talking about McDonald's hamburgers, weren't that great. Well, I had people throwing things on the floor and going, "I've heard enough," and walking out.

Yes, just people walking out, they were furious with what I was saying. And I kept talking. And I finished. And I remember the lady saying, "We'd like to thank Cyndi for coming." And I could barely keep the tears out. And I remember thinking, "I'm not doing this anymore. This is not worth it."

Afterwards, I was walking in the grocery store, and I ran into a close girlfriend of mine. She saw that I was visibly upset. And she said, "What's wrong?" And I explained the situation. And she told her boss, who happened to be Lisa Curry. And I knew Lisa. And Lisa rang me and said, you know, this is what's going to happen. What she ended up doing is she rang somebody else who was doing a ten-day event costing $10,000 for speakers. And she told him. He rang me and invited me to that talk.

Merrian: Wow.

Cyndi: A ten-grand talk, which I couldn't have afforded. And I went to it and was so inspired by these radical thinkers and the amazing people that I kept going. So while I was ready to give up, I then was given the most amazing opportunity.

> *"So I just think when crisis hits, opportunity always comes to you."*

And that was a big, big lesson to me that wait for the opportunity, because it will come. And I have seen that over and over and over again in my career. That was early in my career. And I just keep seeing it over and over. But it's about you making sure that you know where you're going so that the universe knows how to deliver it to you.

Vision and Goal Setting

Merrian: Great advice, I love that. Did that also involve goal setting, because I remember you mentioning that in your talk? And you got us to all write down what our goals were for the next three-month period and what we were going to achieve that. Do you set goals? And how does that help you become the success you are today?

Cyndi: I've always set goals. It's just been something that my parents taught me. I was listening to Earl Nightingale when I was 15. My dad would have him on in the car. And I'm sure at the time, I'd be going, "Oh, could we just listen to some music?" We'd have Earl Nightingale on cassette in the car, in the 1970s. And so I learnt from a very young age about visualization and having a vision and having goals.

And I remember wanting to go to the University of Colorado. And my parents weren't going to pay for me. I had to come up with the money at 19. And I knew that was $5000. Now, you think this is the 1980s. Five thousand dollars was a lot of money. That was just to be a student for

12 months at the University of Colorado. I then had to make $2000 for my airfares. I then had to make enough money to survive the first couple of months until I had found a job. And so I had to basically get $10,000 together in a very short period of time in order to go. And I remember just saying, "Okay, this is my goal. This is what I've got to do." I wrote it all down. And that was the beginning of my goal setting.

Manifesting Your Vision

And then when I met my husband, we did the same thing. We would sit down for a day, and we would set all of our goals. But I think *Manifesting Matisse*, which is a book that I read seven or eight years ago now, where it gave a very step-by-step process of what I had to do. The first process is have a vision.

Second is what does that day look like when you've reached your vision? You know, there were action steps. It was about acting and what are the action steps leading it for the universe to deliver. And so I do those ten steps. And I would do it on a yearly basis now.

Sometimes, if I'm struggling, I will do it as an interim thing. I might do something that I need done in two to three months, and I'll create an interim set of goals.

But I believe that writing it down and doing the actions towards it, even though you think you've done this leap of faith and you think the actions towards it aren't going to get you there, somebody delivers something to you that changes your whole world. And that's basically what happens every time I write this down. Something gets delivered. It just lands in my lap.

Gratitude

And, you know, I do a gratitude journal every single day. And I write in that gratitude journal exactly what I'm grateful for that day, even though I might be crying inside for some reason because things aren't going right. I'd write down the sun's shining. I had a great breakfast. I have a home.

Merrian: A roof over my head, hot water for my shower, clothes on my back etc.

Cyndi: Anything that I could put down, you know, you put down. And I think that we look for the good in life instead of looking at the bad in life. Then the good is going to come to you, because that is the law of attraction, what you focus on, you get. And too many of us focus on the bad that's happening instead of the good that's happening.

Merrian: I totally agree. I was going to ask you what was the biggest single event that impacted your life? Have you already spoken about that, or is there another one?

Cyndi: No, that isn't it. I think the biggest impact was discovering *Manifesting Matisse*, I listened to the author of that book, Michelle Nielsen. And that was, believe it or not, in Chamonix in…

Merrian: In France.

Cyndi: Yes, in France. And I was skiing…well, I was actually speaking at this event. But it was kind of half skiing, half lectures, and I was speaking at it. And she also spoke at this event. And I bought her book. I bought everything she had. And I followed exactly what the book said. And I remember I was at a point in my business where we had decided to take it from just me to I had employed one person, and my husband had joined me. And that's where we were. And that was in 2009. And I thought if I'm going to expand this business, I can't play small anymore. I can't be in my home anymore. I've got to be elsewhere. And I wrote down a leap of faith, a vision of what was in her book. And I wrote down this leap of faith, which I went, "Yeah, right!"

Opportunity

Now, I did that in maybe June. And I went to a talk a couple of months later. And there was this woman talking about this revolutionary protocol that she had found in an old book back in the '70s. And I'm listening to her, and I don't agree with the protocol at all, because it kind of flies against what I believed was my philosophy on diet. I went with two girlfriends. And these two girlfriends decided to do it. And I said, "I'm all for you doing it. And I'd love to hear the results." So I watched. They have been following me and doing what I have been doing and doing unbelievably. But I watched them go from doing amazingly to brilliantly in a very short period of time. And they said… "We have never felt so good." And I went, "Okay, I've got to look into this."

I researched and looked into it and then decided to do the protocol myself. It's based on a book called *Pounds and Inches* by Dr Simeon. And while I didn't agree with everything in it, I manipulated it to make it work in with my philosophy. He had foods in there, probably from the '70s, that I looked at in the year, you know, 2009, and went:

"I would never eat those foods."

So I just substituted with what I believe would work. At this point in my life, by the way, I was hitting 50. I was having aches and pains, putting on weight, which I have never put on weight in my life. I've been, you know, someone that was able to eat the same foods that I had always eaten, because I eat real foods. So there were some things changing in my life.

And I decided to do this protocol. And in three weeks, I lost nine kilos in weight. Felt amazing. No more aches and pains, clarity of mind, no anxiety at three in the morning, which I was starting to get. And I started to go:

"Wow! What just happened?"

Then I started to introduce foods back into my diet. And I realised that the biggest problem of all was weight. It was an elimination diet of the winter foods of the hunter-gatherer. At that point, I wasn't really interested in… weight wasn't my problem. I just decided, well, I'm just going to eliminate it. I'm not going to eat it again.

But I wrote about what happened to me. And I wrote the protocol that I did based on the way I changed it. And our business went out of control, because I had not only written about my experience, but I had created this protocol based on a modern-day type of protocol of it. And our business went berserk. And today, it's our very best seller. It's called the

"4-Phase Fat Elimination Protocol."

We have thousands of people who have done it and succeeded like me. Some of them have taken 60 kilos off and never looked back in their life. And, of course, I needed to study exactly what was happening in the body before I could even write this protocol. So I explained the science behind it. And it was because of that that our business just leaped, which enabled us to move into other premises. We now have 23 people that work for us.

But because of that, then there was a cascade of events that happened.

And one of them, the latest is our documentary *What's With Wheat?* that, number one, I was able to finance by myself. I didn't have to do any crowd funding or anything like that. Number two, it has become a calling card for people to understand or to realise what 'Changing Habits' is. And we have now gone worldwide.

I guess it was that synchronised time in my life that happened that I met Michelle, that I did the leap of faith. And I have done a leap of faith every year since then. And it always happens. We always have this amazing surge. And it's always been about business, always. And just recently, I've just done one for myself to do something with me.

How Are You Paid to Travel?

Merrian: Okay, you've just answered one of my other questions, which was how the documentary film *What's With Wheat?* came about and where the inspiration came from. Thank you for that.

Your work now takes you around the world speaking, sourcing new products for your organic food range. Was travel always a love and a passion? And how are you paid to travel now?

Cyndi: Yes, well, you know, travel has always been something that I've done. My parents instilled that in me. When I was about 15 years old, my parents basically packed up our home and the whole family went travelling around the world for three months. We did England, Europe, Asia. We drove across America in the '70s, in this huge Cadillac. And we drove across America to California and then Hawaii and then home. We did the whole trip in three months. And then my dad had a bus and we travelled everywhere in this bus, so I think my parents instilled in me a love of travel. And, you know, I went to America, to university. I've travelled a lot of the world. I've travelled to Europe, Africa, Namibia and Botswana. This year, I went to Peru.

There's two ways that I am paid to travel.

One way I travel is with my business, looking for foods, doing conferences, speaking around the world. They pay my travel, and they pay my accommodation, and they pay me to speak. I get that opportunity all the time.

Up For a Chat

The second way that I get an opportunity to travel is that I have a podcast called *Up For A Chat*. Every year we go to a new destination and we only take 15 people. It's a very small group that we go with, it's actually 12, because there are three of us who are in the podcast. This year, we went to Peru, and we hiked the most amazing trails. We did the Lares trail, part of the Inca Trail. We didn't do the whole Inca Trail, because we wanted to be away from groups of people. We wanted to be alone on our travels. We went with Mountain Lodges in Peru. And it was one of the most amazing experiences of my life and to meet 12 people that just wanted to travel with us and learn about different cultures.

Next year, we're off to New Zealand. The year after that, we go to Africa, the year after that, Patagonia, and the year after that, Europe. They're expensive trips, because we do it first class. Basically, with regards to when we get there, we want to be well looked after. And we want to make sure that everybody is safe, because we're in places where most people don't go.

And it's those events that we put on that allow us to be paid to travel. That's another way that we do our travel. Yes, I'm always paid to travel. In a week, I go to Tahiti on a cruise. And I'm speaking on that cruise.

And we're doing a documentary on that cruise. The week after that, I'm on a bloggers conference in New Orleans. I've never been to New Orleans, so I'm really looking forward to that.

Merrian: And this is how you are paid to travel.

Cyndi: Yes. And then we do events that we create ourselves. So I travel for those events. So we're in England in March, the US, June, July, August next year. So there's just a few little things we're doing.

Benefits and Rewards

Merrian: Sounds very exciting. You spoke a little bit about taking leaps of faith. And you continually take leaps of faith. For young people who are asking:

"How can I make this a reality for me?"

What are the benefits of getting out of your comfort zone, finding the courage to take some action and to do something differently, because that's what you've done?

Cyndi: Yes, I think what it does is gives you self-respect. And I think a lot of young people have no self-respect for themselves. They abuse themselves with food, drugs, partying. They don't get out and exercise. They think that they're not the best… you know? And I don't know if it's their upbringing. I don't know if it's their peers. I don't know what it is. But they lose their self-respect. And when you lose self-respect, then you don't look after yourself.

If you don't look after yourself, then your brain doesn't work as well. And if your brain is not working as well, your physical body doesn't work as well, because you're not thinking right. And I really feel that when you achieve small things to begin with, then you get that confidence, and you get that respect in yourself and for your abilities and your capabilities. And if your parents haven't given it to you, then you have to give it to yourself.

I'm going to give you an example of my daughter Tarnea. So, she has been bought up in a fairly positive household. She wants to be a world surfer. She struggles to get on a plane and leave the stability of her home. And the first couple of days that she's away, she calls. And I can hear she is upset, and I can see her not doing very well. And I have watched that girl defiantly do that every time she has to travel for surfing competitions, knowing that that's how she feels, she still gets up and does it.

I'm noticing that her respect for herself just grows and grows and grows. And her self-discipline is growing and growing and growing. And her confidence is growing. If she did it the first time and didn't continue to do that, there would be no way she is where she is right now, which is she's at the qualifiers in Cronulla. And so she's just finished round one and gotten through round one.

And I've got to tell you, you know, she doesn't often get past round one in those first couple of years of her surfing. But I'm seeing her confidence grow. But if she'd given up, if she hadn't **pushed her boundaries**, if she hadn't had a vision, and didn't know what she was going to do, I'd say that she would just kind of hang around here, maybe to do a bit of university and maybe eventually get there.

> *"I think if you challenge yourself, you have these visions. You take that leap of faith. You go for it."*

And even if you think it's the worst thing you've ever done in your life, you persist. And what's interesting with a mother and a father with a daughter like this is that I'm the mother that says, "Oh, honey, come home. I'll look after you."

And she has got the father that says:

> *"Never make a decision in a non-powerful state. And you are not in a powerful state at the moment. Therefore, you cannot decide now. You keep going."*

I think you've got to have, you know, the polarization. And you've got to have somebody that's willing to take that leap of faith. And I think creating that vision brings that to you. And even if you don't have that polarization of parents that are there, you can do that for yourself. You can realise that if you're not in a powerful state, don't make a decision. Keep going. Keep moving. Keep acting. And that's another thing my husband always says to her:

> *"If you don't know what to do, just keep moving, just keep moving, just do... do whatever, do something is better than sitting at home doing nothing."*

Merrian: Great advice. Where to next?

Where to Next?

Cyndi: Where to next, well, what I'm doing at the moment is I bought a farm. I bought 60 acres last year. Now, I have to tell you… my leap of faith and my vision that I wrote back in 2009, but I have to tell you, I wrote this vision that I wanted a farm when I was living in the US in 1981. I wrote down I wanted an organic farm, and I wanted animals, and I wanted a food bowl. And I just knew what I wanted. I wanted a health farm. And in 2009 when I did my leap of faith, I then revisited it… I think it was about 2013. And I actually wrote down again:

> *"I want my farm. I want an organic farm."*

And in order to do that, I needed money. I had to have it. You know, I couldn't do it without it, because I don't have the time to farm. I needed money not only to buy the farm, but to employ a farmer who could create my vision.

And so I bought a farm April 6, 2000 and, what are we in, 2016. And we planted 800 trees so far. We have pigs, we have chickens, we have ducks, we have cows. We have a little cottage. We're building a hall soon like for an education centre. And so what I'm doing is I'm creating a food bowl in Maleny on the Sunshine Coast. And we will have farm-to-gate produce, educating farmers and backyard farmers of how to do organic farming and how to do this without having to use chemicals, and eventually, I would like a retreat where people will come and heal themselves. That's probably five years away. But I can see the education centre probably opening within two years and the farm-to-gate within two years. So, yeah, that's my latest project.

Inspired Change

Merrian: Well, we'll stay tuned for what comes after that. But that sounds fabulous. When I heard you speak at Notre Dame University recently, I have to say that the information that you presented was really compelling, so much so that you inspired me to change.

And I have, for the last two, three weeks, changed my habits, changed my diet. And I have to share that the results have been amazing. All

I've done is substitute things, take things out, eliminate things, put other things in. And it wasn't always comfortable. I love my lattes. I had to give up milk. That was very sad.

I was trying every other type of coffee, because I love my coffee and crossword, because that's one of my beautiful daily habits. Each week, I was recording what I was trying this week. And now, I've got to the point where I still long for that latte. But I'm happy with my coconut milk latte now, because I'm feeling great having experienced the changes. And it's staggering. I dropped weight without trying. I'm feeling full without craving food. And I'm stunned and amazed. I wanted to say thank you.

Cyndi: Thank you.

Merrian: Thank you for your time today. Thank you for your wisdom, for the sharing of your knowledge. And thank you for speaking to me.

Cyndi: Thank you. You know what? I wanted... also to say congratulations on acting on that knowledge, because a lot of people are knowledgeable and don't act on it. You are absolutely the hero in this story, because you did something. Well done. Thank you.

Merrian: Thank you, Cyndi.

Key Takeaways:

- Believe in yourself.
- Create a clear vision.
- Don't wait for a crisis to hit in order to effect change.
- Educate yourself.
- Find a mentor to work with you.
- Start out small and out of that big things can grow.
- Have a clear vision of where you want to be and what you want to be doing.
- Set goals and a step by step process to get yourself there.
- Think outside the square and persist with your vision.
- When crisis hits wait for the opportunity to follow it will!
- Do a gratitude journal everyday put your attention of what is good in your life and more will follow.
- Check out Michelle Neilsen's book *Manifesting Matisse*, create a leap of faith, the bigger the better! It will cultivate your self-respect.
- If you are in doubt, just keep going until you move through that doubt and back into a self-empowered state.
- Be the hero of your story – take action.

CHAPTER FIVE

Rising Stars

Mark Cowne

CEO Kruger Cowne, Celebrity Talent Management Agent

"Our greatest glory is not in never falling, but in rising every time we fall."

Confucius

CHAPTER FIVE

Rising Stars

Mark Cowne

CEO Kruger Cowne, Celebrity Talent Management Agent

Merrian: Welcome Mark Cowne, CEO of Kruger Cowne Limited of London, a talent management company, which you started with your wife Gina back in 1998. The company represents some of the world's best-known names, including Sir Bob Geldof, Elle MacPherson, Ruby Wax, Bill Wyman, Dave Stewart, John Simpson, Al Pacino and many others. Since its creation in 1998, when it represented only one or two people, Kruger Cowne has grown into an internationally respected talent management company and currently represents over 320 high-profile personalities worldwide. Welcome Mark Cowne, thank you for agreeing to this interview.

Mark: Hi, nice to speak to you.

Merrian: It's good to have you here Mark. Let's get back to 1998 when Gina called you up to ask you to join her, in what she saw was a great opportunity, and that was representing major talent. Who, were you representing back then, and why did Gina ask for your help to get Kruger Cowne off the ground? What skills did you bring to the table, that complimented her own?

Advertising to Big Game

Gina and I have been married for thirty years this year. We returned to the UK from South Africa where we lived for more than twenty years. My history in business in South Africa, I used to be the Advertising Director and Marketing Director for Phillips Consumer Goods. I then started my own advertising agency. All of my life, I've worked in advertising and PR with some of the big agencies in the UK, and some big PR companies. So, that has been my history and then we progressed more into business, which was our passion. Towards the end of our time in South Africa, Gina and I got involved in a lot of big-game parks, which my wife is passionate about. I sold my advertising agency, and we started investing in wildlife projects.

Anyway, when we came back to England, oddly there was a great shortage of people needing wildlife projects developed in London. Not in Regents Park anyway, so we had to think of something else to do.

Homecoming Blues

It was actually a bit weird that I'd been gone from the UK for over 20 years, and so many things had changed since I'd left. It was very difficult actually coming back to UK. I was coming here almost as much of an immigrant as anybody else from outside the UK. The fact I was born here did me no favours at all. It was very difficult to get bank accounts, because of all the problems there have been with money laundering. My network of really good clients was not around because I'd been in South Africa. I'd been running my own businesses, so that made it very difficult to get employment. The companies that may employ you know you're a maverick and you might not fit in very well to their systems. It was all a bit difficult coming back.

Gina needed to do something to help us, so she started working for John Simpson of BBC. It started with the BBC, and obviously John had massive support from secretarial assistants and things in the BBC, but Gina helped him, with his work outside with his books and meeting engagements and things. John Simpson actually happens to be our brother-in-law, he's married to Gina's sister. So, Gina started working for John on his personal speaking engagements.

Bureaus vs Brands

Gina was talking to people about those engagements, and it started to strike me that the people that she was dealing with would be speaker bureaus. Who actually had no product knowledge at all. They were putting John forward for things, which were really not what his brand was all about. He wasn't enjoying it. It wasn't as good as it could have been for the customer. I just thought it was interesting because this is a very fascinating industry. So, from what I'm seeing of it, and there are a lot of bureaus booking John, they're really unprofessional. They haven't got a clue what John Simpson stands for, what he does, what his value is, what rate he should be getting, just really a bit of a mess.

I said to Gina, you know, we should actually do it ourselves. We should take John on as a brand, as we would have done with an advertising agency, work on those brand values, evaluate them, workout the product life cycle of where he is in his career, where it's going to go, what's it going to mean, you know, when he gets to 65, is he going to be at the BBC, is he going to want to move on, if he wants to move on, how do we do that for him, is that a career in publishing, what is it we do, so we put together a whole new business plan for John, and he joined us.

Value Adding

We then started managing John and putting him out to bureaus, but doing it properly. Saying look, this is what John Simpson is, this is what he's about, this is what he can speak about, this is his value, it's not going to be a discounted amount, and it's not going to be increased over that, we want the thing done properly. And John, suddenly, he was starting to get some really good bookings and ones that he made sense to him, ones that actually required his expertise, stories about where he'd been in the Middle East, what he thought was going to happen, the political risk, in Afghanistan, or whatever. He started telling a lot of his friends with the BBC what he was doing, and naturally within a very short period, we had a great number of BBC people wanting us to do the same for them. Within months we had, I think another six clients, John Sargent, John Humphreys, and it grew. And that was how the whole thing started.

Passion

Merrian: That's excellent. In fact, you've answered a number of questions all at once, I appreciate that. Successful people like yourself are sometimes driven to succeed, and they use the word driven with some conviction, so I wondered what do you consider to be the driving force behind your success?

Mark: **Passion.**

Merrian: Passion.

Mark: Yes, when I look at, I mean, who I represent, global names and it is a passion for that which they do, which makes them successful.

I think this is really interesting, because you mentioned Bill Wyman earlier, who we use to work with, Bill's been a very good friend of mine. When you look at the bands of that era with the Stones and all those people, when Bill started playing with Mick and the boys, he didn't know they were going to be a global success, and multimillionaires, it was just a few boys from around London getting together, because they really enjoyed what they did. They really enjoyed playing and they did it together. Because they enjoyed it, and they were quite good at it, and they remained passionate about it, that made them successful.

That's what younger people today, I may sound like a grumpy old man, seem to miss out on. They want to be instantly successful and they haven't got the **passion** that actually underpins their whole program. They just want to do it, instantly I'll be famous, tomorrow, "Oh how?" "I'll go on television", "Doing what?" "It doesn't matter I'll just go on TV." That's not what it's about; you have to be passionate about what you do. That's the key to my success, you know, you're obviously passionate about what you're doing, and that is why you're good at what you do. If you're not passionate about it, then go home…

The other thing, the other part of it is commitment. You have to be committed to it. It's no good if you're passionate, and then just letting it wash around. You have to really commit to it. Whatever it is you decide to do, do it, get on and do it.

Roving Independence

Merrian: You were born in the UK but you spent 20 years in South Africa. I just wondered about growing up, what lessons did you learn growing up that helped you, become the success that you are today?

Mark: My parents weren't overly engaged in my growing up, so I think that I learned to be independent at very early age. I realised that they weren't going to do it for me. In fact, it's interesting, because, I've lived all over the world because my father was an air traffic controller, and he used to get posted to weird places like Bahrain, or Uganda or you know, wherever, and I'd end up sort of moving around, or even within the UK.

As a child, it's incredibly disruptive, because just as you're starting make a new group of friends, you're suddenly up and you're off again to somewhere else. You start all over again, and you're always the new boy in the class, new boy at school, it's a different school, syllabus, whatever, so it's all very disruptive and confusing. I had to start just spending time very much on my own, because I had very few people around me. I didn't have a friend support group at school, I had very little support from my rather confused family, so I'm very independent. I think independence is good and I think it's bad. I think there's a degree of independence, which actually is not good. You do need to have something or someone that tempers that independence or you can't grow up completely dogmatic.

Merrian: What do you mean by tempers it?

Mark: Well you need somebody to argue back with you. It's no good you saying this is how it's going to be, this is what it's all about, and not actually having anybody around you who tempers it and says, well actually, that's really interesting, but have you really thought about so and so?

Merrian: Ah.

Mark: Too much independence does tend to make you dogmatic, which I think is a dangerous thing to be. I think you always have to consider other viewpoints and opinions; otherwise they just dismiss it and go do it anyway.

Early Dream

Merrian: If I was talking to the teenage Mark, you were obviously living in various different places, what would he have most wanted out of life? Apart from probably chasing pretty girls and driving racing cars. What did you dream of doing with your life?

Mark: What did he dream of doing, or what was he doing?

Merrian: What did he dream of doing?

Mark: Actually, it's really strange, because, for the whole of my life, I was going to go in the army, and that was it. It was a very clear-cut decision of what I was going to do. I was part of the Army Cadet and I was part of the combined Cadet Force at my school. I got quite a good rank in both of them, and it seemed like an interesting life to me, with lots of travelling around, meeting interesting people, hopefully not killing all of them, and it was quite interesting. I got accepted for Welbeck Officers Training College to be a Royal Engineer Officer, and at the time they accepted me, I also got accepted to Portsmouth College of Arts.

Big Decision

This was a very big decision in my life because art had always been a hobby of mine, and something I was interested in. The teenager in me thought I could go and be an officer in the army and command a thousand guys or so, and be posted all over the world with these guys, or I could go to Portsmouth College of Art, where the really pretty girls were, and there were lots of drugs in the common room, alcohol in bar, and I thought, well actually, the army can bugger off now, art is where it's at, and is where I've gone wrong. So yeah, I was good at art and choose art college.

Merrian: It's an interesting dichotomy really, from one extreme to the other. Being very artsy and bohemian to very disciplined and regimented in the army. Not sure what the army would have made of you?

Mark: No, it would have been a disaster.

Merrian: You would possibly have been kicked out?

Mark: If there had been career advisers, in the very early stage he probably would have said to me, Mark, you really shouldn't be going into the army.

Merrian: Aside from chasing girls, drinking beer and the drugs, was the education in graphic design training useful to you in your advertising agency?

Art College to Advertising

Mark: Well, I did my diploma in graphic arts and design, and I spent three years doing something, I can't remember completely what. Nobody ever can of course, because it was all good fun. We had great fun, and we all passed, so I think actually the teachers were on the same drugs as us so no one knew what we were doing.

I went and got a job at Lonsdales as an illustrator, and I was all right. Then I got promoted, I got another job with another agency somewhere, I can't remember who they were, a low-lying agency, and when I was with the other agency, I started to realise that I'm sort of okay at this, I'm not bad, I'm still quite good at retouching pictures. I'm not bad at illustration, but the thing is, I'm not brilliant.

There were an awful lot of really brilliant people around me, so I realised I was going to never going to make it to the big agencies, and work on the really big accounts, and crack the really big salaries, because they were always going to be better than me. But what I did find was I completely understood the entire process, so I was very good at managing creative people.

Management and Power

They were brilliant, absolutely brilliant people, they were creative and absolutely the most disorganised people you've ever worked with. But, I understood them, so I was able to manage them and run an advertising department, a creative department, at a very early age.

I realised my talent was actually managing things more than necessarily doing them. Beyond that, I got posted away from there by a client company, who wanted me to go into their organisation and run their advertising for them, so I would then be working with the ad agencies, because I understood how they worked and where the savings could be made, and how to actually get proper briefs done. I actually found out I was really good, so I really enjoyed working for client companies because it was a position of power. The agencies had to do what I wanted them to do, and it wasn't me being pushed around by the customer. So it was quite cool.

"Leaders don't create followers, they create more leaders"

Tom Peters

Challenges

Merrian: These are really good skills to take with you into what you're currently doing, which is dealing with creative artists, dealing with, what I imagine are sometimes big egos, and they all require a different skill set to how you manage them. What are some of those challenges that you had to face, and how did you meet those challenges?

Mark: The challenges are exactly that, which you say. When I used to run the advertising department for Phillips, I used to work with our sales force there. Every day the sales force went into the office, that old clock radio was exactly the same as it was the day before. The talent I manage today, it's never, ever the same. We represent 320 people, and they're not ever the same any day. It is completely empathizing, understanding, predicting those sorts of mood swings, patterns, and problems and dealing with those, which is just unlike any other product range in the world. I've got a catalogue in front of me on my desk I'm looking at now with 320 products in it. In my case though, those products are people.

Commitment and Inspiration

They have a completely different brand values, product life cycles as anything else.

Merrian: Going back to the army and discipline, are there any rules that you've had to develop that have actually stood you in good stead when dealing with your client base?

Mark: Well, be professional is the one that just really, I insist on completely. Is that whatever it is we've agreed on, we've committed to, even if it was wrong, we going to have to see it through. We've committed to it, we're not going to let anybody down, and that's not going to happen. That is actually why we don't represent a couple of people anymore, because they let people down, and we had to let them go. I can't tell you who they are, obviously. The one was married to Mick Jagger and recently married a very rich in Australian. I can't tell you her name. And the other one is someone who swears a lot, I think was on TV, was Scottish by background, but I can't tell you his name, Gordon Ramsay, either.

Merrian: Working closely with inspiring people, aside from those you no longer work with, I'm curious to know what inspires you?

Mark: In fact it's quite an interesting question, I'm inspired by success, but that doesn't have mean Rupert Murdoch type of success. It can be my receptionist. As long as anybody who achieves something notable, in any way, I find really inspirational. If you are succeeding in the things you set out to do, that does inspire me. I'm greatly inspired by someone's commitment to things. Geldof, who is someone I know really well, and I've worked with him for a long time. I'm always inspired by the commitment that Geldof made to the people of Africa and poverty, and you know, thirty years later he's still as involved as ever, and that is well, and I think it's a great commitment and very inspiring.

Goals

Merrian: It's very commendable. You just talked about goals, many successful people often set goals. Do you set goals for yourself, and what were the first ones that you set for yourself, and when did you achieve them and how?

Mark: Get laid at art college, and that happened in about the first week.

Merrian: Okay. A bigger goal maybe, that took a little longer?

Mark: That was pretty enormous, that goal. I tend to set a lot of business-related goals. I set very few personal goals. Business goals are always sort of get the people on board that we want to develop the business, to run a more effective business. Do what we can for the community. I haven't got any magic sort of goal setting process or anything.

What I do always think is really important is to **set realistic goals**, even for yourself. I've none of this I'm going to make ten million before the end of the year. You know, that's just not going to happen. How about if I increase my turnover, my income, by 15%? That's achievable, yes I can go for that. I run a lot of marathons, and in that, I always find if I set a goal for that, firstly my goal is to finish the marathon, not in any particular time, the thing is I want to finish it. If I do a good time, that's a bonus, but the goal is to finish it. My goal always is to step by step finish the marathon. To do that extra step is just one more of 42,000 steps you're going to take.

"Everything is possible if you take it in bite-sized pieces."

The Lows

Merrian: Good advice. Sometimes we learn from our mistakes, it's not just from our successes. Have there been any lows that have taught you some lessons, and what were those lessons and experiences?

Mark: Yes, I've had a few lows. I think anyone running their own business would agree with me on this, is to be successful in business you also have to be unsuccessful in business.

You know, it's very unusual just to walk in and suddenly everything in the world is brilliant. You need to have some failures as well as successes. I've had good businesses, I've had bad businesses, I've made lots and I've gone bust, so in all those things that you learn an awful lot from it.

The one thing I really have learned:

> *"Be very cautious of who you depend on when things are going wrong."*

I've noticed both with myself and others around me in similar positions that when things start to go wrong and you start to become more desperate, you start listening to and taking advice from people that you would not normally even give them the time of day. Because you're so desperate, you think they're going to bring you a solution, of here's your last resort, oh my God, you know, he can really do it, wow he's going to do it. The reality is, no he's not, he's still useless. Don't do that, just cut whatever your losses are and move on. Don't compound them by listening to idiots.

One Young World

Merrian: Often people have a bigger vision. Is the involvement with **One Young World** and the **Rising Star** program, and I really encourage you to talk about why you got involved in that, is that part of what you consider to be your bigger vision, your giving back?

Mark: Yes and no. **One Young World** is interesting. One Young World started, I think it was about ten years ago, and they initially came to us for some really mega names, and it was being run by a woman that had actually begun with us as an agency, and it all sounded really goodie, goodie and highly improbable and the sort of level of people they were looking for from us, was incredible.

The really bizarre thing was, they weren't really looking for them to be speakers, they were looking for them to be counsellors, and they felt that the importance of One Young World was the empire summit is actually about the young people, about the youth, because they are the **future leaders** in business, politics, religion, sports, whatever, you name it. And we shouldn't be talking down to them from our viewpoint because we screwed it all up anyway. What we should do is provide them iconic names at the event that would give credibility and gravitas to the event. It's quite an interesting concept.

They came to us for **Jamie Oliver** and **Bob Geldof** and a number of very high profile people. When we went to the first one, which was in London, I think we went there with sort of trepidation, thinking it was going to be a disaster. When we started speaking to some of the young people there, the first thing we noticed, was they had hundreds of countries represented. Then the next thing we were talking to these young people, and they were fantastic, **some were 25 years old and running three international companies**, and we thought these people are incredible, really interesting young people. We bought into the idea and have supported it ever since.

Finding Solutions

Oddly, rather completely bizarrely, is that the woman who runs it, Kate Roberts, used to be my paint director in South Africa, when I was with Phillips and she was with J. Water Thompson, some 35 years ago. We've known each other a rather long time, and we are very much behind it, and over the years we've seen it develop. It went from I think, 105 countries to 120 countries, and at the last one we had 190 countries represented, which I think means only three actual, official countries in the world were not there, which is incredible.

What we really enjoyed was we were seeing the young people trying to find solutions to things that bothered them, from all over the world. We saw groups of them getting together petitions to present to the UN, they were going to lobby and bring about change. Proper seriously coherent things and this wasn't just during One Young World event, this continued through the entire period afterwards.

We really thought this was an exciting idea, and we liked it so much, it toured around the world, and most countries bid for it, they don't bid for it financially but they bid for it in terms of what they're prepared to do to make it work easily within their city. It's been to Zurich, Pittsburgh, Johannesburg, Dublin and Bangkok. It really is fascinating it kept touring around like this. It's really a good project.

Rising Stars

When I started to think about, where are the future leaders going to come from? Where are my next clients going to come from, who's going to be the next **Bob Geldof**, **Dave Stewart**, **Joe Walsh**, where are they? How do I find them? I thought a really good way of doing this would be to run a program with One Young World, which not only has 2000 people going but a broad reach to, 15, 20, 30, 40, 50,000 more beyond there, and to see what's there, who can we spot as being next of these amazing people.

We developed the **Rising Star Program** where we give a trip into space to somebody who could actually tell us why that would be important to them. What they would actually be able to use that platform for and how

that would benefit what they are trying to achieve. It is a great, (excuse the pun) launch pad for something you want to do. We had thousands and thousands and thousands of entries, so many incredibly interesting, brilliant young people. Which is great, from a business point of view, I've got great database of all sorts of talent I can be watching and see where it goes.

Finalists

It came down to, three contestants who were very impressive – a young Nigerian doctor, who committed himself to go and work in the Ebola clinics with no regard for his own well-being or safety. Knowing that, he stood as much chance as anybody of dying from Ebola as a result. Next was a very brilliant young Irish woman. And then there was Manawer who, as you know, did actually end up winning. These three were judged at One Young World by some One Young World organisers; some of our directors, and the One Young World people themselves, the delegates.

I think we probably would have picked a different winner, but when Hussain Manawer got on the stage, and spoke about his concerns and views on the need for more attention to mental health, it just blew everybody away, it was incredible, that's all it is. Mental health is one of the key things that's really effecting the world today, and subsequent to say winning the prize, we kind of want to work on this, and we're going to work with Hussain, and put together a very large mental health summit here.

Merrian: Awesome.

Mark: It is, it's an amazing thing, that one in four people will definitely be touched or have been touched by somebody or have had a mental health issue. That's quite a lot when you think of six billion people in the world. That means more than a billion people actually have some sort of mental health issue, and that can be from really significantly dangerous to actually very remedial.

It is a bit of giving back, it becomes that. I think, initially, it was more of a commercial decision, but obviously it is a star project for us now.

What's Next?

Merrian: Well Mark, you caught the pretty girl and you married her, you drive the fast cars, you're putting the next generation of young leaders into orbit. Is there anything else on your agenda or in your goal setting? What's next for you?

Mark: Now that's an interesting one, I forgot about that, that's actually rather important. This is a very strange scene, but a few years ago I was in Qatar with Bob Geldof, and I ended up going to a party where, in Cher's words, she was my date for the night, which was interesting. We've actually become quite good friends. We've realised that there were oddly some things that we had in common. I can't remember off the top of my head what they were, something to do with England making her career with Sonny, and me being interested in wildlife, she's quite passionate about animal welfare. Anyway, so that was a few years back.

Then recently, I get a call from **Cher** saying what do I know about this elephant in Islamabad being brutally treated, it's in a bad zoo and the elephant's name is Kaavan. I said I don't know anything about it, but maybe I should find out. It's true, it's an awful story. Twenty-eight years being chained up in a zoo, really horribly treated, so I think okay, fine. This has got to stop, I've had enough of all these stories with Sea World, and zoos and everybody doing dreadful things with animals that really just shouldn't be happening. It's gone beyond its time, we don't need them anymore, we don't need to be doing individual research, so I've got a bit of a bee in my bonnet.

Virtual Zoos

I decided what we'd do is, Cher and I would put together a major campaign to try and overcome the torture of these animals in captivity. That's one of the things that we are doing, and that's something that I do feel quite good about. I've been to Islamabad, I've gotten Kaavan unchained, I've improved his way of his life. We got Kaavan sorted to a degree. I'd like to get him free and put in a sanctuary now, but he's one of millions of animals around the world whose lives this applies to. **We want to bring about change**, we're going to do a massive thing together, which Cher and I will release when One Young World is in Ottawa. It will call on the young of the world to help us put pressure on government to ensure that anybody who is involved in zoos does do something with proper standards.

If zoos are not doing it, they should be closed down. The biggest goal is going to be to actually bring about change of the younger generations to stop supporting these things, where it's humiliation and torturous for animals. We're working now with Samsung and some other people, where we can start creating virtual zoos. Kids don't want to go out anyway, so make the most, as a matter of fact they're crying now, if you want to go and checkout the animal, here he is, put on your Google goggles you can see him without sticking your nose in the zoo. That's a little thing, which in some ways, good or bad I may end up getting remembered for. I don't care if I am or not, it doesn't bother me, but it is something I do feel is something worthwhile that I'm trying to do.

Merrian: I think it's a wonderful project and I applaud your support for it. Mark Cowne, thank you very much for your time today, it's been a real pleasure talking to you and I really appreciate the time you spent with me.

Mark: It's been lovely to be with you. Can I just say just one last thing about our little project? The reason I agreed to do this with Cher, was I realised that we, as people can, have the most unbelievable network of people around us, that I could entrap into assisting me with this. I've got Dave Stewart who can actually can write songs, I've got John Landau who can make videos, I've got Cher who can sing, I've got people in the World Wildlife Fund who can support us, I've got PR companies, I've got you name it, I've got the biggest network of people ever. I suddenly land one day and say, okay, you're going to come support us with this, and remarkably they all said okay, so that was what made it happen, and I think that's what being clever in management is about, it's really absolutely understanding and identifying and using the most resources, the best we can.

Merrian: Beautiful ending, thank you very much.

Key Takeaways:

- Do what you are passionate about if you want to be successful.
- Take Action and get on and do it.
- Be independent not dogmatic.
- Find what you are good at and do that.
- Recognise where the positions of power are and seek them out.
- Be professional.
- Whatever is agreed on, be committed and do that, even it its wrong.
- Set realistic achievable goals.
- Use celebrity to bring about Change, e.g. Bob Geldof's commitment to Africa. Cher's commitment to animal rights and the freeing of mistreated animals.
- Use your resources to the best of your abilities for the greater good.

CHAPTER SIX

Steel Heels to Stilettos

Sharon Warburton

Telstra Business Woman of Year, Chairperson, Mentor and Founder of Steel Heels Foundation

"Never allow a person to tell you no who doesn't have the power to say yes."

Eleanor Roosevelt

CHAPTER SIX

Steel Heels to Stilettos

Sharon Warburton

Telstra Business Woman of Year, Chairperson, Mentor and Founder of Steel Heels Foundation

Welcome to Sharon Warburton. I'd like to begin our interview with a little of your background. Sharon's achievements are many and to list a few, the 2014 WA Telstra Business Woman of the Year, 2015 NAB Women's Agenda Mentor of the Year, mother, and founder of Steelheels.com.au, a foundation that's dedicated to the promotion and advancement for professional working women.

Sharon has lived and worked in Australia the UK and in the Middle East. Sharon's CV is not a resume many would attribute to an accounting background necessarily, and she's a frequent user of Twitter where she's mostly seen wearing a hardhat and high visibility clothing, which is unusual attire for the Chairman of the Board. But appropriate for her positions in the mining and construction sectors.

She ranks her achievements as being a mentor to many, workplace flexibility champion, and gender pay gap elimination campaigner. Sharon's work has taken her to view mineral sites and diamond mines in places such as Southern Africa, Quebec and the Mojave Desert in California. She's experienced exciting helicopter rides in PNG and Indonesia, lived and worked in London, Abu Dhabi and has worked with a number of major international companies including Multiplex, Citigroup and Rio Tinto. She's currently a non-Executive Director of Fortescue Metals, Western power, Wellard Limited and Gold Roads Resources Limited. Welcome, Sharon Warburton.

Sharon: Thank you.

Accounting to Steel Heels

Merrian: Sharon, you studied to be an accountant. The view of you on mining and construction sites wearing high visibility clothing and steel capped boots is unusual one for an accountant. How did your journey to corporate success begin, and what was life like growing up?

Sharon: I grew up in a small country town in the northwest of Western Australia called Exmouth. And as a kid, the most exciting thing to do was to get on every sporting thing you possibly could because that means you got to go away and travel to other towns in the region to compete. And so for me, many of those towns were the mining towns in the Pilbara and that was incredibly exciting. As a small child and a teenager, I got to see those big mines, and I think that's probably where the seed was sown, and that one day I'd loved the opportunity to work for the big companies that owned those mines.

Merrian: Successful people like yourself are often driven to succeed. What do you consider to be the driving force behind your success?

Sharon: Both of my parents worked for as long as I can remember, and they worked really hard. And I think from a very early age… from when I first entered the workforce, the one thing I remember is my folks telling me that hard work drives success. It's the lesson from my parents, and it was that sort of message from my parents that I remember being the driving force to my success.

The Six Cs to Success

Merrian: Beautiful. Having had the privilege of speaking to you before, I'm aware that you identified what you like to call your six Cs to success – can you please tell us what they are and how they worked for you and why you recommend them to those that you mentor?

Sharon: When I reflected back on both my personal and professional career and also the work I've done as a mentor, what I discovered was success could be defined in six categories. And conveniently, they all start with a C. Those six categories are:

- confidence,
- courage,
- commitment,
- can-do attitude,
- communication and
- creativity.

If I just reflect on each of those, my experience is when people are confident in their own ability. That confidence tends to lead to a success.

A lot of my work, I focus on working with emerging leaders to increase their **self-confidence** in the work place and in doing so helping them create success. I think that's the number one, most important of the six Cs.

The second one is about **courage** and courage can take many shapes and sizes and mean different things to different people. For me, it's having the courage to try different things to have my seat at the table to have a voice, to be able to speak up and certainly over the course of my career

it's also been to have the courage to walk away from opportunities or roles when things weren't right.

The third one around **commitment,** I guess it's summarised as you're either in or you're out, and there's no such thing as in between. And so, from my experiences, success comes from whatever you want to try by giving it 110%, not just dipping your toes in the water expect them to be a success.

Number four around the **can-do attitude**. It is best summarised as when you focus on the positive it's amazing how opportunities will reveal themselves. And I certainly can point to a number of times in my career when I focused on the positive, new opportunities have emerged.

Fifth one is around **communication**, particularly in male-dominated industries. I hear feedback often where people aren't communicating as well as they should.

In my view, a problem shared is a problem solved, if we can increase the communication in those workplaces, then perhaps we can reduce the rates at which young women, in particular, are leaving male-dominated industries. And we can use that as a way of reducing the gender gap.

And lastly but not least, it's important to be **creative**. And again, summarised probably best by saying when we are creative and **invest in ourselves**, we can make our own opportunity and create our own successes.

Too often, I hear people are just sitting back waiting for other people to do it for them. I think key to my success has been to create my own opportunities. And in one case, I even created a role for myself that didn't exist in the entity at that point in time, but it was a wonderful opportunity for me to get some experience in areas that I hadn't done before. **I created my own opportunity**. That's a success, and that's why I think they work.

Travel the Great Teacher

Merrian: I remember I've heard you say this before, that one of the things that you said about yourself was that **you backed yourself**. And I think that's what you mean by courage and confidence in thinking that I can do this. But often, women don't speak up and don't say I can do this. They sit there and think they could do it, but they don't necessarily communicate it well. It's great to hear you say that, not only did you back yourself by communicating, you actually ended up creating that role for yourself and that's a great incentive.

Sharon: Yes, I agree with all of that, too often we don't back ourselves, and we invest enormous amount of energy in the negative in creating thoughts around why we can't do something and not as much around the positive as to why we can do something. My view is if we put that same amount energy into thinking about creating opportunities, we'll get greater success. And I still, even today, I hear myself sometimes thinking the negative, but the good thing is that I recognise that and stop that and turn it into a positive.

Merrian: Having that awareness is a great achievement. As a teenager, what did you want most out of life? And if I asked that teenager what would her answer have been and has that changed for you today?

Sharon: As a teenager, I wanted to travel the world.

Merrian: I find that perfect for my book!

Sharon: And I know that's changed today and it's still a massive motivator for me in everything I do and being a mother today, I'm inspired to travel and take my daughter with me so she can experience the world from a younger age than I was able to.

Merrian: Yes, travel is a great teacher, I believe.

Desire to Travel

Sharon: And I've reflected on where that might have come from because I went to a country school, didn't have television as a small child. I can't put a direct trigger on it, but I wonder whether there was some sort of book or something at school in the very early days that inspired me to understand what the rest of the world was like.

Merrian: Exactly. For me, it was a book when I was seven, and my third-grade teacher introduced me to the library. And I discovered the book called *Anatole of Paris* and Anatole was a little mouse who lived in the sewer of Paris, and he was determined to travel the world and everybody laughed at him and said he can never do it. And quietly, he just thought very determinedly, I just won't stop. I won't tell them I'm going to do this, but I'm going to do it anyway and he set about making it happen. And as a seven-year-old, I began to journey with him to Istanbul and Paris and Rome. And it was at that young age, that I decided that's what I was going to do with my life. Travel the world and have lots of adventures!

Passion

Sharon: Yes, I don't remember something as powerful as that, but I do remember there were some things going on. For example, I had a little trouble with my eyesight when I was a small child, so I got to go on an aircraft first to go to the hospital to get my eyes checked. And I remember that being incredibly exciting, travelling on a plane so that might have been part of the desire to travel. Also, the town where I grow up at that stage had a very active US navy base. So there was a lot of children in my class came from the US and I was so fascinated by what they did, it was so different to what we did. I wondered whether that also triggered a desire to understand what the rest of the world was like.

Merrian: Some of the other people I've interviewed for the book have rated passion as the number one trait that they look for in employees, and I'm just wondering how you rate passion and what it is that you are most passionate about?

Sharon: Passion is important, but I wouldn't have put it at number one. There's a couple of things. I don't think there's a clear number one for me, but a couple of things come into mind around trust and honesty, and also underlying intellect. Certainly, inner passion would be up there, but it's certainly not a clear number one in my opinion.

Merrian: Okay, is there a single event that impacted on your life that changed things for you, and what was that?

Sharon: Hard to think one, but there has been sadness, I think, in my life which has made me realise that we need to live everyday to the best we possibly can. And that probably led me to change my focus from being the workaholic that we all imagine to leading what I'd call a natural balanced lifestyle.

Merrian: Feel free not to answer this, but if when you say sadness was that grief due to a loss?

Sharon: Yes.

Merrian: Yes okay.

Sharon: Of family and friends.

The Big Break

Merrian: What about opportunities then? Was there a big break or an opportunity that had a really big impact on your life and changed your trajectory in anyway? And what did that opportunity look like?

Sharon: I began my career as an accountant, accounting graduate at KPMG, and after completing my chartered accounting qualification, I went backpacking around the world for three or four months. And I realised that a chartered accounting firm wasn't for me. So I went for a job interview with Hamersley Iron, which is now known as Rio Tinto Iron Ore, and the people that interviewed me remain friends today, and they said I was terrible in the interview, but they saw potential in me, so I got this job. I often look back on that as a big break or an opportunity, and I often wonder if I hadn't received that opportunity what might have happened.

Merrian: And what you'd be doing today, possibly?

Sharon: Yes, the opportunity or the biggest break was people recognizing a talent under the surface. I think that was when **I was 24**.

Merrian: Wow, that was very young. And it's lovely that people have that sort of faith in you and you responded well, obviously.

Sharon: Yes, I think it's the opportunity we need as leaders to create, and then let the people shine through. Sure, let's lead them and guide them, but let's give them a chance. Too often people don't get opportunities, and I had a couple to kick start my career, and I grabbed to them. I do, as a leader, really focus on creating opportunities wherever possible, giving people a chance.

Merrian: I think that's the trait of a leader, isn't it, to be able to allow the space to allow other people to shine?

Sharon: That's right.

Merrian: People who aren't necessarily leaders are fearful of the people coming up underneath them, tend to squash people down because they're afraid that they might overtake them. But a real leader can step aside and say go for it, do the best you can and let's see what your capable of.

Sharon: That's right. I truly believe that there's room for us all, whether in the current organisation we are working with, or within the community at large, if we have that confidence I talked about earlier. Then we're confident that there's room for us all, there's room for opportunity for us all and that is what I think we should be creating here.

The Low Point

Merrian: Exactly, and sometimes we learn more from our mistakes than our successes. Are there any mistakes or times that you can point to and can remember thinking… Well, I really learned a lot from that experience. Can you share some of them with us?

Sharon: The low if I can describe it as the low in my happiness meter, was my time in the Middle East, and that was because this was the first time in my career where I was in an organisation where I didn't feel my colleges or my peers valued me and I found that a very difficult situation, so I wouldn't say it was a mistake so much as it was a challenge and a low of point in my career.

Merrian: Having lived in the Middle East, I completely understand those kinds of challenges.

Sharon: There's one thing I do know and that is I'm not perfect and I make a mistake every day. And if I can be conscious of everything I'm doing every day and constantly trying to learn from those, however small they are, or however big they may be, then I think that's a good space to be in, as opposed thinking that I don't make mistakes.

Merrian: Well I think we all need to take responsibility for our own actions, and yes, we all make mistakes and sometimes owning them is part of what makes us grow.

Sharon: Yes, that's right. I agree.

Goal Setting

Merrian: Are you a goal setter? What were your first goals and when did you achieve them?

Sharon: Yes, I set goals on a daily basis before I go home every day, the goal for the next day. I set challenges for each year. Might not be on New Year's Eve, but certainly, I will have some goals. I will have some longer-team goals. I'll have some three-month goals. I like to go on holidays once every three months. I usually will set myself some goals around that period as well. Yes, I'm very much a goal setter. When did I first set goals for myself? Well, I actually set goals for myself in high school.

Merrian: That doesn't surprise me. Do you remember what they were?

Sharon: Yes, achieving certain marks and giving myself the opportunity to get in certain courses. There would have been goals around sports. I was a swimmer as a child, so there were goals around achieving a certain time, certain races.

Merrian: Would you call them personal-based?

Sharon: Yes.

Merrian: Rather than the need to beat somebody else, was it more like I need to improve on your own past performance?

Sharon: To beat my own time, yes. I was never the best, but I was always motivated to do better than I'd done before.

Merrian: Yes. I think that is all any of us can do, and say:

"Well I might have stuffed up but next time, I'll do better!"

Sharon: Yes.

Benefits and Rewards

Merrian: Being a great traveller and being motivated to travel and work that takes you to exciting places, can you list what you think might be the benefits and the rewards that you've enjoyed by taking those leaps of faith and backing yourself, having the confidence to step up and create opportunities for yourself? What are the benefits and the rewards that you've enjoyed?

Sharon: I'm able to combine my desire and love for global travel with work. That's been a huge benefit and reward. Whenever I travel for work, I've been able to take on some explore time, but also time where I've been able to immerse myself in the culture of other parts of the world. The benefits and rewards also extend to accelerating my career and as a full-time non-Executive Director by 45 years of age, there's not a lot of other females that achieved that. And I was only able to achieve that because **I took those leaps of faith** and grabbed opportunities through my 20-year corporate career before that.

Giving Back

Merrian: So that all comes to backing yourself and taking those risks. But I like to call them calculated risks. People say to me you're a risk taker, and I go, "No, I take calculated risks, provided I actually think, yes, I can do that, and I back myself."

Sharon, you also hold a number of not-for-profit directorship, namely with Princes Margaret Hospital Foundation, Curtin University Business School, an emerging leader in philanthropy program. Can you tell us little about that work that you do and why you take on those roles?

Sharon: It's an important part of waking up every day, is to identify how I can use my unique skills-set to support organisations that don't have an unlimited budgets. And the ones that I'm particularly passionate about are reflected there in Princess Margaret Hospital Foundation. Obviously, I show the passion around the health and wellbeing of children, which as a mother, is really important to me. As a small child, I spent lots of time in Princess Margaret Hospital with my eyes, and so it's wonderful to be able to give back now as well.

Empowering Women

The Emerging Leaders in Philanthropy Program is for the Princess Margaret Hospital Foundation. In doing that piece of work, I'm trying to create mixed generational philanthropists and increase their awareness of the work that the children's hospital here in Perth does, and create that bond and connection between now and emerging leaders in the children's hospital. Curtin University Business School I work in two areas, one's around the Asia business centre, and the other is my love of cross-culture and globalization, I think, they are the drivers there.

I'm Curtin alumni with where I did my undergraduate degree. There's a desire to continue to support Curtin University, and I'm also the patron for their Women in MBA program. That program, in particular, provides scholarships to women who wish to undertake the MBA because we're not seeing as many women as we see young men undertake their MBAs. As a passionate campaigner about creating opportunity for women I'm delighted to be able to do that through Curtin University Business School.

Merrian: I always find it interesting what people choose to support. In your case, you've supported things that you've grown up with and is now important in your life because you were a child patient at Princess Margaret. And now you've got a child who possibly will need those services. It's wonderful to see your commitment and support for these organisations. How would you like to be remembered?

Do What You Love

Sharon: It's not really something that motivates me, to be remembered by others. But it would be kind of cool if my daughter, Chloe said I was a good mother. And when you asked me that, the number one thing that comes into mind is, I don't do what I do to be remembered for something, I do what I do because I love doing it.

Merrian: Sharon Warburton, I really appreciate your time. Thank you so much for speaking to me today, thank you for agreeing to be included in my book.

Sharon: Great, look forward to reading it and I appreciate your time.

Merrian: Thank you.

Key Takeaways:

- confidence,
- courage,
- commitment,
- can-do attitude,
- communication and
- creativity.

- Set personal goals. Make it your intention to do better next time.
- Recognise talent and foster it by mentoring those under you.
- The mark of a true leader is one who can foster talent without fear of being exceeded.
- Believe there is room for us all.
- Back yourself and your belief that you can do it.
- Do what you are good at, and offer those unique skills to organisations in need.
- Value the people you work with.
- Ask for what you want particularly women in corporations.
- If you never ask you'll never get.
- Set yourself challenges and keep motivated.
- Do what you love. Love what you do.

CHAPTER SEVEN

Flying High

Graham 'Skroo' Turner

Billionaire, Philanthropist, and CEO Flight Centre Group

"The ultimate truth about business is that there is no ultimate truth."

Graham Turner

CHAPTER SEVEN

Flying High

Graham 'Skroo' Turner

Billionaire, Philanthropist, and CEO Flight Centre Group

Welcome Graham 'Skroo' Turner, the CEO of the Flight Centre Group and one of its original founding partners. You began your adventures as a bus tour operator around Europe back in the late '70s and since then you've navigated the Flight Centre Group to the success that it enjoys today. Currently, Flight Centre Group employs 20,000 people, has 3000 retail outlets across 14 countries worldwide, is that right?

Graham: Yes, more or less. Our sales are about $20 billion and we have 19,000 or 20,000 people working with us. We have shops and our corporate travel teams. Of those 3000 teams probably about 1800 or 2000, are physical bricks and mortar shops and the other 1000 teams could be in the corporate, wholesale or other areas.

Merrian: I would like to start back at the beginning if I may. You grew up in Queensland, and there's a story in Mandy Johnson's book *Family Village Tribe* where she describes you as a young boy, learning to ride a bike. And the way you did that was taking yourself to the top of a hill and hurtling down at great speed and being stopped by a wire fence, but you kept going until you learned how to ride the bike. Do you think that early childhood experience in learning to be self-reliant is part of what makes you a success?

Early Years

Graham: Look, I don't think it hurt. I think that story came from my elder sister, actually. We lived in a fairly isolated spot, about 10–15 miles west of Stanthorpe on the Texas Road. My sister and I went to a one-teacher school, which had about 40 kids accommodating all eight years of primary school. So you ended up riding through the bush, basically. I think we were about six kilometres from the school. With only one teacher, it meant you just had to make the most of things, so you could do them on your own or you didn't do them at all. I think it was generally a good experience.

Merrian: Actually speaking of good experiences, one of the underlying things that came through in Mandy Johnson's book was this idea of let's have some fun, so having fun in the early days with Top Deck, involved lots of drinking, lots of parties, and lots of taking risks as a young man. What does fun look like to you today?

Graham: It's certainly a little bit different. We started Top Deck in '73 and started Flight Centre in about '82. The risk taking in Top Deck was simply the time of my life; then I was in my '20s. I'm afraid the sort of risks, as well as the sort of fun we had then, would be probably not quite be the right way we'd do it today. I don't think we'd get away with it. If we consistently did it, probably we would end up in jail!

Work and business should still be fun and as an organisation even with nearly 20,000 people, I think most of the people who work in our group in 14 different countries would say that generally, we have fun.

It's not all easy, some of it's difficult, sometimes results aren't what we'd want, but overall I think there's still that focus on enjoying ourselves and having fun. Once we've finished a hard year or even a hard week, mostly it is about having a bit of partying and enjoying ourselves, as well as learning on the job. **Personal development, learning skills and other things, are an important part of our work place.**

Personal Development

Merrian: And that really intrigued me, that personal development was part of the process of your development of the company. You introduced personal development into that culture and offered it to your employees, which is really commendable.

I just want to take you back for a minute, back to, being known as unconventional and a bit of a rule breaker, probably stemming from those fun days at Top Deck. Having read about the risks that were taken and rules that were broken, it appears you only defied rules that defied common sense and that weren't necessarily in the public interest. That said, do you have any personal rules that you live by today?

Graham: Well, yes, I mean, I've got a family, only a small family, son and daughter and my wife Jude. I think we enjoy ourselves. We try to make sure that we keep in touch with the kids. We have the odd holiday with them, the odd meal with them. Jo lives in London so, that gives us an excuse to get to London a bit more and obviously, we have quite a large business there as well. Personal fitness and health is really important. I think it's important to stay healthy as a family. I suppose, it's living your business life a little bit like your personal life, but obviously they're quite different and quite separate, too.

Be Passionate

Merrian: One of the other things that underpins the attitude within the company culture seems to be an absolute belief that you placed in all of your consultants and they responded to your belief positively, by being very productive. Are there some common attributes that you can identify in your most successful consultants, or if I phrase that another way, what makes people the success that they are? What were you looking for when you hired them?

Graham: In terms of people who come into our leisure shops initially, it is generally people who are passionate about the role, passionate about travel. We have quite a reasonable size bike business with 28 retail shops in Australia. It's the same there. People need to be passionate about riding bikes so they can pass this passion on to customers and customers can see it. That is quite important. It's the same for travel. If people come in our organisation and they don't really love travel, love the destinations they're talking to customers about, it just doesn't have the same effect. That's a really important part of it.

Merrian: Where did your passion for travel come from?

Passion for Travel

Graham: I grew up in a pretty isolated orchard, and I can assure you it was pretty boring. Then I went to boarding school in Toowoomba, and then university, I did vet science at University of Queensland. It was always one of the things in the back of my mind, and not only myself. I think a lot of the friends I went to school and through university with, we had basically the same ideas that we were all going to travel.

In 1972, a bunch of friends and I went to the Munich Olympics and travelled around Europe. We just really enjoyed it. After long periods of studying and having a good time there, not having that responsibility we had at university, for maybe six months travelling around Europe just cemented in us that this is one of the things that we really enjoyed doing and went on from there.

Merrian: That's great, because I also share that passion for travel. You successfully restructured the company as it grew and then you broke it down, interestingly, into families, which were teams of seven, villages which were teams of three to five, and then tribes which were teams of 25.

Positive Leadership

You had some tough years in the '90s with the Gulf War and with SARS, and then you discovered that the teams that held positive attitudes were actually recession-proof. But those that actually didn't have the positive attitude, that had a negative one, thinking it was all doom and gloom, they actually lost money and it was a bit of a self-fulfilling prophecy. So, if they believed that they would succeed they did, and if they didn't they failed. How do you promote this positive attitude in the company now?

Graham: We're quite a large organisation now, but we still keep the basic parameters. Teams of four to seven people with a team leader, and we have some much larger shops but they might have five teams in one shop, for example, with five team leaders. And the villages, as you said, three to five or six teams under a village leader. That's generally a team leader as well. Areas or tribes generally consist of, as you say, 15 to 20 shops.

A lot of this is about leadership; a lot of it is about positive leadership, and positive attitudes to customers and the people you work with. And there's no doubt that in a recession, when things are not going well, if you can really promote the fact that there are opportunities around in these sort of times, I think it's really important.

After September 11, we had to put in a lot of effort, by promoting ourselves through advertising, that's what we did then. It is one of those things that we try to counter what would normally happen and generally there's a lot of positives come out of that.

Fun

Merrian: If I had met the 23-year-old you, who was backpacking around Europe and asked you what you wanted most out of life, what would your answer have been and how has that changed for you today? What would you want most out of life today?

Graham: When I was 23 when we started Top Deck out of London, fun was a really important part of our life, as was socializing, travelling with other like-minded people, not worrying too much about money. We generally managed to find enough money to enjoy ourselves, to eat out at cheap but good restaurants whenever we felt like it. Saving money was the least of our concerns. At the end of the day, we had to run a business. Basically, it was either spent on the business or on having fun, and those were about the only two things we really concentrated on.

Merrian: What about today?

Graham: Today obviously, business is quite large and quite successful from our point of view, most of the time. I still enjoying my work, having fun, both with my family life and in my business life, is really important. I still enjoy physical activity, doing a reasonable amount of bike riding, play touch football, go for runs, and that sort of thing, so that's still an important part in my life. Circumstances certainly have changed, but I think I still enjoy the same things.

Merrian: That's good to hear. You're quoted as saying:

> *"Start with a lucky break. Have a clear dream. Stay focused and passionate about achieving your dream."*

What was your first lucky break? And were there more to follow?

Highs and Lows

Graham: I think there's obviously been a few downsides, but from when we started in business in '73, and the Flight Centre in '81, sure there's been ups and downs, but I suppose, generally, we've been lucky in being able to survive some of the downturns. We had serious cash flow issues in the late '70s when we basically invested into too many buses without having access to enough cash. We were lucky to survive that. Mainly with the help of particularly suppliers, whom we managed to negotiate an arrangement with when cash was really tight, then things came back quite strongly in the early '80s. I think in '95, when we floated on the ASX, we did it for different reasons, basically because we wanted to give our staff a chance to be able to buy into the organisation. I think that was a really good move and that made us a lot more professional organisation.

Certainly when we first came into Australia in 1982, our biggest lucky break was that the retail travel industry was just starting to be deregulated. Before that it was illegal to discount, so we were a bit of a disruptor at the time. We were the first group to really come in and discount airfares heavily without getting prosecuted by the government. And built our business up pretty quickly to the end of the late '80s and early '90s. So, in that sense we were in the right place at the right time.

Rewards and Recognition

Merrian: The Flight Centre also has an ethos that supports philosophies that are inherently just and gives reward and recognition where warranted, and that motivates people to achieve more than they thought was possible. At the age of 23, what did you dream that was possible and have you exceeded your own expectations?

Graham: Look, it's one of those difficult things to look back on. I remember I was working as a vet in Brighton, I think, in the UK, probably early in 1973. I had this idea of having double-decker buses travelling around, with people beds and kitchens on them, because I had seen a couple around Europe during our travels. I was never satisfied with just having one bus and one trip. However, I did envision even before we started that we'd have a lot of buses running all over the place within a few years.

I think the same thing when we started in Flight Centre in 1981. I didn't have a clear long-term picture of where we would end up, but I was always an empire-builder myself. And I think I managed to convince any of the partners I had during a period that this was a good idea as well, without necessarily having an end destination in mind.

We do work a lot more on our longer-term planning now. We're looking at 2035 and where we'd like to see ourselves being by then. Whether we can actually do that and achieve that, you can't see into the future, but certainly that's one of the things we aim for now.

Merrian: I think you've consistently proved that if you believe you can, you can.

Road Blocks

Graham: Yeah, but there'll be road blocks that come along the way, too, and the world changes. You know, in 1995, when we floated, there was basically no internet, or it was just getting off the ground, and it's had quite a profound effect in travel and in other areas, mostly areas of business.

Merrian: Well I know that your first foray into the internet was not a wonderful experience, but you've returned to it recently. You have now got Top Deck back in the fold, I believe, and you've also made a recent acquisition of Student Universe, which is another online business. And that's with an eye to fast-tracking the growth in the youth travel sector. Do you have any advice for student travellers setting out and wanting to travel the world and also to find ways to be paid to do it?

Student Universe

Graham: Look, there are a whole range of different ways that people can be paid to travel, and I know that there are a range of different blogs that people can contribute to and generate content that you may be able to get paid for. We're certainly getting more involved in online, and Student Universe was one of our recent purchases. It's one of the most successful online travel booking services. It's based in Boston, but obviously we'll be growing it. It is available in Australia, but we'll be growing that a lot in the next few years.

I think it is one of the things in business, you can't do everything perfectly and you've got to focus on things that you're good at and really make sure that you can take that to the level that you want to take it to.

You just can't be good at absolutely everything, but we're getting a lot better at our online opportunities as well as our bricks and mortar shops. And that's where we see the future. And even for students, when students are travelling, we have a Student Flights brand with about 80 shops in Australia and still a lot of young people when they're travelling, like to get advice from people who've already done it themselves. It's not just a matter of booking an airfare online and heading for Europe. You can get good advice from a brand like Student Flights, who can give you, some of the things that you can look at doing while travelling as well as working overseas.

Benefits and Rewards

Merrian: Brilliant, so, for young people who wish to follow in your footsteps and who might want to embark on a journey of fun and travel, can you share what are some of the benefits and rewards that you enjoy from taking those leaps of faith? Top Deck was a leap of faith. Getting into the internet was a leap of faith. Setting up the bricks and mortar shops was a leap of faith. Grabbing those opportunities when they present themselves – can you just, outline some of the benefits and rewards that have come from taking those opportunities when they presented themselves?

Graham: Yes. When you go to university and I'm not sure how most people treat university, but certainly when we went to university, the vet degree took five years. We were mainly interested in, I suppose, enjoying it, learning all about life as much as actually getting a degree. I think the same thing is when you're travelling. Certainly it's about seeing things that you want to see, some of the famous sights of the world, but it's also about how you meet people, how you get ideas, how you think about things.

> *"It is easy to be a big fish in a small pond, it takes courage to leap out of the pond and swim in the ocean."*
>
> **Merrian Styles**

I think that's why travel is such a great experience, just as I think the right to a university education is too. I don't think it's about necessarily just seeing great sights by travelling, or just getting a technical degree by learning in the university. And I think those are the things that really set you up for the future to give you the opportunity to visit the areas that you probably wouldn't have thought of, if you had stayed at home and got a nice, sensible job.

A Bigger Vision

Merrian: Exactly, travel is a great teacher. You learn a lot from travelling about other cultures and being exposed to different ways of life and different ways of looking at things. Lastly, I'd just like to ask you, you're a regular runner and a bike rider. You love the Australian bush. Do you have a vision that's larger than yourself, a philanthropic one or a goal of any kind or do you have a legacy that you would like to leave behind or how would you like to be remembered?

Graham: Yes, both my wife and I are passionate about wildlife and trying to save our environment. We have a couple of reasonably large properties and we've got a couple of cattle stations about an hour west of Brisbane, and along with the University of Queensland, we're building quite an expansive wildlife breeding program that will be run by the University of Queensland on our property with a breed and release program.

We are trying to bring back some of our endangered species in southeast Queensland. We're quite passionate about that. I think it's one of the

most important things that we can do for future generations, is to try to save some of the animals and birds, in this part of the world, that are becoming quite rare, everything from koalas to quolls and certain types of cockatoos. That's really the legacy we would like to leave and our kids are quite interested in it too. So future generations can really enjoy a restored environment and wildlife.

Merrian: Graham Turner, thank you very much for your time. I really appreciate it and so will my readers.

Graham: Thanks very much.

Key Takeaways:

- Do something you love to do.
- Do what is FUN and you will never work another day in your life.
- Set goals and believe in yourself.
- Be persistent and be positive.
- Reward and recognise good work.
- Look after your staff, treat them like family, believe in them.
- Take care of your staff, they will take care of your customers.
- Employ people who are as passionate as you are.
- Make personal development a priority, offer it to staff and management alike.
- Start with a clear dream, stay focused and passionate about your dream.
- Have faith in yourself and focus on what you are good at.
- Be an empire-builder, have a vision bigger than yourself.

CHAPTER EIGHT

Committed

Karl E Watkin MBE

British Businessman of Year, Serial International Entrepreneur

"All that is necessary for the triumph of evil is that good men do nothing."

Edmund Burke

CHAPTER EIGHT

Committed

Karl E Watkin MBE

British Businessman of Year, Serial International Entrepreneur

Welcome, Karl E. Watkin, MBE, thank you for agreeing to this interview. As a serial entrepreneur, chairman, and inspiration with a solid track record for bringing new technology businesses to the international marketplace, and with over 30 years' experience of living and working in Asia, you chaired the UNF Bio Energy Advisory Board and co-chaired the UN White Paper Review on climate change, and were a member of the Clinton Global Initiative, to name just a few of your achievements.

As an influencer and difference-maker, and with so many achievements at your disposal to choose from, what do you rank as your greatest achievement to date?

Karl: Surviving losing 130,000,000 pounds sterling.

Merrian: Well, actually creating the 130 million pounds and then losing it?

Karl: Well, no, surviving losing it. There are not very many people who can say they survived losing 130 million pounds.

Merrian: That's true. I believe you grew up in Newcastle a middle child in a working-class British family and, like many entrepreneurs, left school at an early age to pursue a career. What did you do in those early years? And how did you get from a school dropout, to British businessman of the year?

Early Years

Karl: I left school on the Thursday, and I started work on the following Monday and sort of merged into working for United Biscuits, and that was in 1974. Twenty-four pounds a week and a company car. I had the choice of two jobs. One was a salesman without the company car. The other one was a merchandiser with a company car. Both paid the same. So I took the company car route.

A merchandiser is basically someone who priced biscuits and put them on the shelves. I worked for United Biscuits for three years, become a trainee salesman, and then my boss… who was a key accounts salesman, had nervous breakdown. For the last nine months that I worked for them, I had to do his job. Not only did I do his job, but I increased his figures massively.

For some unknown reason, the company, when they came to replace him, they didn't even interview me for the job. I was furious about it. Then virtually the same day, HJ Heinz the can makers, wanted a key account salesman for the same area, with the same customers. They were interviewing the following week. I didn't apply for the job, but I got asked to go for an interview, and I went for the interview, and I got the job. So I left United Biscuits and went to work for Heinz, as a key account salesman.

At the same time, I was a DJ, seven nights a week, and I ran market stores on Saturday and Sundays. Eventually when I was 23, I decided that it was time I got serious with my life. I packed up the DJ job, packed up the market stalls. Before I did, I went on holiday, and was in a hotel in Moscow, and I bumped into a guy who seemed to have a great job. He was the international marketing director for Combine Harvester. I asked him about his job. It sounded fabulous. He got to travel all over the world, free of charge.

About three days after I got back to England, there was a job advertisement in the paper for a trainee export manager with an engineering group, and you had to have a degree in engineering, five years' capital equipment sales experience. You had to be able to speak fluent German, fluent Spanish, and fluent French, and there was something else. There were six things, and I had none of them. But because I wanted the job, I applied for the job anyway, which I would encourage anybody to do. I was amazed when I got an interview. I was even more amazed when I got the job!

I got the job, packed up the market stores, packed up the DJ job, and focused my attention on university, doing a business degree by part-time. I started working and travelling overseas, at somebody else's expense.

Merrian: Well done.

China Years

Karl: Then in 1981, I went to live in China for about three years. Well, in 1985, China just about went bust. I hadn't realised that my sales in Asia and China were about 90% of the company's turnover. When China fell over, it meant that the company was in serious trouble. The reason the company was in serious trouble is because they hadn't modernised their product. It was still the same product that was designed in the '40s. It was 50 years old, basically.

Then I got offered a job as a sales director for a company in Cambridge and another job for a company in the Middle East as managing director. I decided to take the managing director's job in the Middle East, went

into work to resign. My boss said that I couldn't resign because if I left, he couldn't retire, but this was the first conversation that we'd ever had on the subject. I told him that, "Well, today's the day. If you make me sales director today and you retire, fine, I'll stay. But if you're not going to do that, I'm going to take the job in the Middle East." So he retired, and I got his job and then discovered why I had his job, because the company was losing £8000 a day!

Taking Over the Company

I put a plan together to save the business by developing a new machine, and it's a bit of a long story, but they didn't want to modernise. I set about getting rid of all the people who were standing in the way of modernization, by getting them fired. Then I went to see Sir David Pasco who was chairman of the company and he said the plan was great, but they didn't want to do it. I said, "That's fine. Will you sell me the company?" He agreed to sell me the company for £1.4 million, which, because he was losing £8000 a day, was quite entertaining.

So I bought the company and started running it like a market store and started designing a new machine, so I designed a new machine within nine months and got it out in the market. I took the company from employing 130 people worldwide, to employing 1650 people worldwide, sold it for £20 million in 1993. Then I took five years off and sailed around the world in my yacht *Commitment* and had a lot of fun.

Then I came back and did it again and again and again.

Mind of a Millionaire

Merrian: You participated in a BBC series called *The Mind of a Millionaire*. In that series, experts uncovered interesting qualities of entrepreneurs, like yourself. Some of those qualities were they're **focused**, **creative**, **imaginative**, **competitive**, **determined**, and they also have an unshakable belief and confidence in themselves and their ability to deliver. Are these characteristics you would use to describe yourself?

Karl: Yes. I think I would agree with all of those things, but the biggest thing that's a characteristic of all the people that were involved in that series, and I think there was eight of us in total. Mostly they had the things that you talked about, but the one thing that we all shared in common was that we were all lazy. Because we were lazy, we were focused and, therefore, only did things like made a huge difference.

If you said to anybody that knows me really well that I was lazy, they would just laugh out loud because I'm not. I work really hard, but there's a difference between working really hard, for example, as being a postman for 60 hours a week and delivering letters, or working 60 hours and making £50 million, and I'd rather do the latter than the former. Well, I couldn't do the former.

Merrian: In that series, one of the entrepreneurs said, "All entrepreneurs are not lazy. They actually work really hard." So I don't understand why you say you're lazy?

Karl: If you give entrepreneurs the option of somebody dropping a million pounds a month through their letterbox, they would have just stayed at home and had fun… that's the difference. Everybody works because they have to work. Entrepreneurs, because they're lazy, they're therefore very **focused** on what they do.

Learn in the Jungle

Merrian: In the same series, **Sir Richard Branson** was quoted as saying, "Entrepreneurs often leave school by 15 and learn in the jungle how to survive, and those survival skills are what determines their success." Do you agree with that statement? And what survival skills did you learn?

Karl: That's absolutely true. I followed in the same league. When I was 15, I went to Spain, and worked as a waiter. Then I ran my market stalls until I was 23, selling on a Sunday in the Edinburgh markets. If you can sell on a Sunday, to the people of Edinburgh and Glasgow then you can sell anywhere in the world. That's true.

Do What You are Passionate About

Merrian: I've also heard you say, "I only do what interests me, and if it doesn't interest me, I pass on it. Then it has to be fun." Can you share some of the fun you've had in creating so many successful IPOs? And what does fun look like now? And why do you consider fun an important ingredient in what you do?

Karl: Well, life is very, very short, as we're both very aware. If you're not having fun, what's the point? I had to go to Sydney last week. Sitting in a traffic jam, first in the morning and last thing at night, and I'm looking at all the people sitting in the traffic jam, and they're there for an hour and a half a day, in the morning and at night, three hours a day, sitting in a poxy traffic jam. What the hell for? Three hours a day. That's 15 hours a week. That's 750 hours a year. You're sitting in a car, being miserable, travelling to and from the office. I couldn't do it. I'd rather gouge my eye out with a rusty fork.

You have got to leap out of bed, charged and be delighted to be doing what you want to do. I mean tonight is an example. Tonight, I'm jumping on a plane, as you're well aware, and I've got a 23-hour journey. I'm straight off the plane, and I'm straight in institutional presentations in London when I get there, because what I'm doing, I really believe in. Right? I'm going have a lot of fun doing it. Of course, a lazy man wouldn't do that. A lazy man would just stay here in Australia and sit on the beach. Obviously I'm not lazy. Obviously I'm going to have a lot of fun. I just wouldn't do anything that wasn't fun.

Rule Breakers

Merrian: Entrepreneurs are also known to be unconventional and rule-breakers. Many find operating within structured systems and organisations, like schools or academic institutions, unproductive. In the *Mind of a Millionaire* series, most entrepreneurs were discovered to enjoy being in control. When others are in charge, they didn't thrive, and they either opted out of the game altogether, or they changed the rules so that they could win no matter what.

Karl: Yes.

Merrian: You led a high-profile campaign to free the NatWest three and you also led a campaign to repeal the extradition treaty to the USA. These are examples of where you've worked to change the rules. What motivated you to lead those campaigns?

Karl: Because it's fundamentally wrong. The extradition treaty was actually brought in after 9/11 to extradite terrorists to the United States. It was unfortunate that the two guys that I actually ended up defending were alleged terrorists. One was found not to be a terrorist, and one was a terrorist, but that's not representative of the type of people that have been extradited by the US.

Actually, they don't have to produce any evidence. You just have to say they suspect that there's a crime, and off they go. Gary McKinnon was another classic case and suffered from Asperger's. Gary was a successful case. We managed to arrest his deportation order and the extradition order.

Only this week in the UK, another identical case, with another kid about the same age, who's also got Asperger's, is being extradited to the United States for hacking into computers, to face a prison sentence of 99 years. Whereas in the UK, he would get something like three years if he was found guilty, versus 99 years.

> *"We shouldn't, first of all, be subcontracting the UK judicial system to the United States. If somebody commits a crime in the UK, then they should go to court in the UK, and if found guilty, they should go to prison in the UK."*

I believed it to be the right thing to do. It's just farcical there are six times more people in America than there are in the UK. You would expect the UK to extradite six times more people from America to the UK but that's not what is happening. The American girl, who was found not guilty, then guilty of killing the English girl in Italy, America refused to extradite her to Italy. I see that as hypocritical.

I believed it was the right thing to do. I'd crossed the river for a fight, and I would do it all over again, despite the fact that I proved in the High Court in London that the Metropolitan Police, the CIA, the FBI, the Crown Prosecution Service for ten years all lied to the court. They still extradited the guys.

When they got to America, having spent two years in solitary confinement, one of them was found not guilty, and the other one, had they been found guilty, having spent twelve years in prison – ten years in prison in the UK and two years in prison in the United States – was returned and is free. It's just an incredible story. Here we go again, with the latest young guy having Asperger's.

Believe in yourself

Merrian: Next question. There seems to be an underpinning attitude with most entrepreneurs, an unshakable belief in themselves and what they can achieve, is that unshakable belief what drives you and drives your success?

Karl: Two things everybody says about me. One is they're very frightened of me for some reason, and I can never understand why anybody is frightened of me, because if I ask you to do something, and you do it, then I'm delighted. If I ask you to do something, and you don't do it, then I'm pissed off. If I ask you to do something, and you say you'll do it and don't do it, but you tell me, that's okay. That's about the limit of my judgment on people. The second thing they say about me is that I take huge risks, and I've never taken a risk in my life.

Every single thing that I do, I know exactly what to do and how I'm going to get it done. That's the difference between me, and a lot of other people, and the difference between entrepreneurs and other people and it was bought into sharp focus four weeks ago in London. We were trying to list some gold assets that we have worldwide, and the two other guys made a list of all the reasons that it couldn't be done. It was quite a long list. There were about 12 things on the list. They didn't even want to get started on it. Whereas the 12 things that were on the list, I looked at them all and went, "I reckon I could find a way around most of them." I didn't see them as a barrier.

The difference was I would go ahead and start knocking them off. They wouldn't go ahead... They wouldn't even start because it was going be too difficult. And the result is, the meetings that I'm having in London tomorrow is because I'm going to go ahead and deal with it.

Break Down Barriers

Merrian: It's rumoured that when you moved from Sales and Marketing Manager of Crabtree and you bought the company, as the new owner, one of the first things you did was to reconstruct the company canteen by taking a sledgehammer to some of the walls and knocking the walls down between the directors, executive, and workers canteen divisions.

Karl: Yes.

Merrian: Sounds to me like you make a habit of knocking down walls between people. Because you've just knocked over those 12 objections by saying, "They're not objections. I could find a way around those." What did you achieve by breaking down those walls?

Karl: Well, it was two things that I did on the first day. One was that all the best car parking spaces were reserved for directors and they had their names on them. So I pulled them all up, and I put a notice up. It was quite frankly because there used to be a funny TV program set at Butlins at the time in the UK, called *Hi-De-Hi!*

Merrian: *Hi-De-Hi!*?

Karl: *Hi-De-Hi!* Yes. So the manager of this establishment was called Joe Mapping and he used to send notices to his staff, saying, "Now get this you lot…" I started doing all the notices to the workforce, saying, "Now get this you lot. From here on in, the first one in, in the morning gets the best car parking space." It worked, and people started coming in early in the morning to get the best car parking space.

Unions

Here's the difference between being in sales and marketing and becoming the managing director. I had to deal with the trade unions, and the trade unions had a convener. We sat around the table, and they said, "We want a pay rise." I said, "Well, you're not getting one. We are trying to save the company and you're not getting one."

Then they had a second meeting and third meeting. The third meeting, they wanted to go to something called 'outside conference'. Well, I didn't know what an outside conference was. Outside conference was we all went to the trade union. We had more conversations. Well, it was nothing whatsoever to do with what was going on with my company. I said "no" we are not going. They said, "Yes, we are." I said, "We're not." I said, "You might go, but I won't be going to that." I said, "We're going to sort this out here, and the bottom line is you're not getting a pay rise. Ask me when the company can afford to pay you more. Then we'll pay you more. I suggest you go away and think about it."

The next morning, they came back, and they said, "We're going to outside conference." I slapped my hand down as hard as I could on the desk, and I just said, "You're not listening. We're not going to outside conference," and I got up and walked out. Right? Now that could have gone two ways. They were threatening the company, and they were threatening me. They could have walked out, and I would have found a new workforce. Yes, I gambled, and it wasn't a risk. It was gamble on

the fact that my reputation was SO good in the company because I was very, very well liked. The workforce wouldn't support the trade union. And I was right. They didn't. We never had, in all of the time that I was in charge of that company; we never had another union meeting.

Merrian: That's certainly an achievement.

Karl: It was good. I looked after the guys as well. They ended up very well looked after, my guys and I treated them like my own family.

23-year-old

Merrian: If I'd met and asked the 23-year-old you, what would he have wanted most out of life? And today, what do you want most out of life today?

Karl: If you'd asked me what I wanted out of life when I was 23, it was very clear. I wanted a Porsche 911 and to have paid for my house by the time I was 30. Seven years later, I had paid for my house, and I had a Porsche 911. Then of course, you buy a bigger house, and you buy more cars. Eventually I ended up with 17 cars and a 650-acre estate with five houses and a big chalet in the French mountains and a chateau in the south of France.

If you ask me now, what I want is what I've got, a beautiful view on the beach here in Fremantle, a lovely, comfortable bed and every now and then, I have to go back to Europe to work, and I really don't like that very much. I wish I could do everything from here, and I'm trying to make that happen.

Commitment

Merrian: I've noticed you often use a quote from WH Murray, the leader of the Scottish expedition in Nepal in the 1950s. The quote reads,

> *"Until one is committed, there is hesitancy, the chance to draw back, always ineffectiveness. Concerning all acts of initiative or creation, there is one elementary truth, and that the moment one definitely commits oneself, when providence moves to, all sorts of things occur to help one that would otherwise never have occurred. A whole stream of events issues from the decision, raising in one's favour all manner of incidents and meetings and material assistance, which no man would have believed would have come his way. Whatever you think you can do or believe you can do, begin it. Action has magic, grace, and power in it."*

Why does this quote resonate with you? And in your experience how has commitment been influential in your own success?

Karl: Well, there are two sayings in my life. That's one of them, and I'll tell you about the other one in a minute, and that I got from an American training course called 'The Forum'.

It was something I really believed in, if you don't commit yourself to getting something done, it's just not going to happen. Once you commit yourself to doing something, all sorts of things crawl out the woodwork to help you.

Its been my experience, that all of my life, once I committed myself to doing things, everybody's there to help. Things just happen by magic. They help make it happen. It's just amazing, and I'm so convinced of it, that I named my 50-meter yacht that I had for five years *Commitment*.

I had 'Commitment' etched in the windows to my house. The other thing I had etched in windows in my house is another saying I very much believe in, which obviously supports what I did on the extradition treaty, and that is,

> *"All that is necessary for the triumph of evil is that good men do nothing."*
>
> **Edmund Burke**

Biggest Impact on life

Merrian: Couldn't agree more. With a multitude of choices, what do you consider to be the single largest event that's impacted on your life so far? And how did it change things for you?

Karl: Well, I think the biggest thing that changed my life was when I got expelled from school, when I was just 13. I lived in a very working-class area, a ship-building town, called Walls End which is the rough end of place called Newcastle, which is the rough end of England. So it wasn't a very great place to live. My parents were absolutely appalled because my father was a policeman in the town at the time, and it was appalling for him. It was just a disaster. I was the black sheep of the family.

Anyway, we ended up going and living in a place called Morpeth. When we got to Morpeth I thought I'd died and gone to heaven because it was such a lovely place to live, and the people were really nice. I thought, "**Well, if that's the worst that can happen in my life. I'm going to start pushing the boundaries**." That just encouraged me to push the boundaries in life, and that's what I've done all my life, and I'm not going to stop now.

Merrian: Bravo.

Karl: That's had an impact on every single thing I've done.

Exceed Your Own Goals

Merrian: Do you have new goals to achieve over the next five years? When you set those early goals, which you achieved, do you think you exceeded your own expectations?

Karl: When I used to publish our annual results at Crabtree I used to say what our profit was going to be for the following year.

Merrian: Yes.

Karl: I used to put it in print, a year before we made it. Of course, we always made it because you said you were going do it because you had committed yourself to making that profit. So you somehow made it.

Merrian: Do you think you exceeded your own expectations?

Karl: You always exceeded what you set out to do. One year, we set ourselves the target of turning over $100 million, and with 24% profit, on, on, on, on. We failed. We got to $95 million and 23% profit. Of course, all the smart-asses were saying, "Oh, we're a failure. Yeah." Well we grew the company from turning over $3 million to $97 million in seven years, with a 24% compound, year over year, growth and profit and turnover. Yeah, we're a real failure.

Merrian: Doesn't sound much like a failure to me.

Karl: Wasn't a failure to anybody it was just a joke, an absolute joke. It was great. I mean the other thing about Crabtree was we had to change the whole environment, in which the company operated. Another first, was I gathered all of our competitors and got them to work together. There were 200 machine makers, and I got them all working together to a common agenda. That was not easy. As chairman of the World Can Making Machine Manufacturers Association. I chaired it for five years and set up a world exhibition because we never had an exhibition before.

Getting everybody to agree to a common agenda was really hard. But I did it. It was good fun. I really enjoyed it. The most fun I ever had in my life was running Crabtree and the World Can Making Machine Manufacturers Association. It was a hoot.

Benefits and Rewards

Merrian: If young people were wishing to follow in your footsteps and embark on a journey of fun and travel, can you share some of the benefits and the rewards you enjoyed by taking those leaps of faith, grabbing those opportunities, and having that unshakable belief in yourself?

Karl: Well, for 37 years I have travelled all over the world, in private jets, in private yachts, in first-class planes, business class on planes, staying in the very best hotels, staying in the very best places, and mostly somebody else has paid the bill. I've done a lot of crazy things as well. Most of those I probably wouldn't do again. But it's been absolutely fabulous. There's no question about it. I thoroughly recommend that people travel and get somebody else to pay the bills.

It's a different world for kids today, though. I grew up in a world where there were differences. For example, there were differences between the information that I had available to me, and the information somebody in India or China had available to them. That's not the case today. It's a much flatter playing field.

Indeed, Chinese kids who are 25 and Indian kids who are 25, with the same qualifications, are much hungrier than they are in the UK, or they are here in Australia. It's a much more competitive world. To be honest, I don't believe that young people today can do anything other than travel. They used to say that travel broadens the mind, but **you can't do anything other than travel because that's where the opportunities lie**. They don't lie in your hometown. They lie in getting together with the very best people worldwide and making sure that you are one of them.

Merrian: That was actually validated in that BBC series by the young man… Dominic McVey who was called 'the scooter boy'. He was supposed to be at school one day, and they saw him on the Tokyo television, investigating different kinds of toilets, that he thought he was going import. He didn't stop himself from getting on a plane and going to Tokyo to check them out, and he was 17.

Karl: How old is he now?

Merrian: Not sure. He made £7 million by the time he was 17. He's doing pretty well. He made his money importing scooters, but he was off doing the next thing.

Next question: Do you have a bigger vision, something philanthropic perhaps?

Philanthropy

Karl: Well, the philanthropic work I've done it because I want to do it. My work for the UN, which I've paid for by myself, a lot of people would promote that as philanthropy, but **I did it because I saw real**

opportunity to make a big difference. That's all I was interested in, and it was a lot of fun. It was really entertaining there, kicking around with the global leaders of the world for five years. I couldn't believe it. I used to sit, thinking, "How the hell did I get here? A lad from Walls End!"

Putting money into a charitable fund, so that we could help charities in England, that was essential to me as well as I was asked all the time to give money to good causes, and it was much easier to just, say, deal with the charity, deal with the trust all the time. That got rid of the problem for me, which is another angle on being lazy. You know? It wasn't common knowledge I had the trust, and still isn't common knowledge.

Again on philanthropy, fighting the extradition orders. That cost me about £400,000 in total over the years, and that's philanthropy as well, but I didn't do it for philanthropic reasons. I did it because it was something that I believed in.

Merrian: Is there anything I haven't asked you, that you'd like to be asked or that you would like to add?

The Forum

Karl: Yes, I want to just tell you about the training course, called 'The Forum'. It was amazing because I was thirty. I went on this course, it was really astounding to be in a room with 60 people for so long, talking and having in-depth conversations about anything that anybody wanted to talk about.

One of the first things that I discovered was about consensus. With 60 people in the room, when one person asked: "Would it be possible to turn the heating up? Because I'm too cold." I said, "Yes, I'm too cold as well. I'm pleased you said that." The guy in front who controlled the conversation, he said, “That’s an interesting question.” Now, I would have died for the fact that it was too cold in that room. Right? He asked anybody who was too cold to put his or her hand up. I’ve got my hand up, and I look around the room, and not everybody had their hand up. I thought, “What the…?”

He said, “Anybody here too hot?” Now 15, 20 people put their hands up because they were too hot. Then there were 15, 20 people who were just about right, and then there were some people who couldn’t make their bloody minds up, which is typical. Then I just thought:

> *“If 60 people in the same room can’t agree what temperature it is, what chance have we got in the world of getting agreement on anything?”*

There were lots of things that came out of it. It was real good, including the commitment quote.

Another thing that came out of it was, and I was really ashamed of myself over this. There was a guy who looked like a complete plonker. But he seemed to be doing a lot of good stuff and getting a lot of things done. I asked him if I could go and work with him for the day, and he said, “Yes, that’s no problem at all.” He was about three hours away by car. I drove the three hours, and I went to work with him for the day. He was just amazing. Absolutely amazing.

At the end of the day, I thanked him, told him what a great guy he was and how I really enjoyed the day, and he told me that I’d spent a lot of my life writing off people who can make a huge contribution, but they would make that contribution in different ways, different than I would normally do myself or the way that was expected.

> *"Therefore, I learned that I could get really good performance out of everybody in the team if they were allowed to get on with it."*

A classic example of that is when I worked at Heinz. I was there for 24 months, and I was United Kingdom's top salesman for 23 to 24 months, bearing in mind that I left the company in 1979. I had the world record for the world's biggest-ever sales of Heinz goods to one store. To my knowledge, in 2016, 37 years later, that record still stands. But Heinz had this rule you had to be at work at 8:30 am in the morning. You couldn't leave until 5:30 pm.

During my time there of course I was not there at 8:30 or at 5:30. They were actually going to sack me (despite me being the UK's top salesman) for not being at work at 8:30 and 5:30, when what they should have been doing if they had any brains, was to find out what it was that I did between 11:00, when I got to work, and 3:00, when I went home, and made everybody else in the company do that. You know?

Merrian: Karl Watkin, thank you very much for your time.

Karl: No problem at all. I shall see you and speak to you later. Bye for now.

Key Takeaways:

- Be focused.
- Be creative.
- Be imaginative.
- Be competitive.
- Be determined.
- Have an unshakable belief and confidence in yourself.
- Have an ability to deliver.
- Think outside the box and see opportunities where others see objections.
- Treat your workers/colleagues like they are your family.
- Don't write people off because they operate differently instead allow them the space to get on with it.
- Back the people who do what they say they'll do.
- Get rid of those that don't.
- Push your own boundaries.
- Whatever goals you set yourself put it in writing.
- Educate yourself attend training courses.
- Seek out mentors.
- Don't write off people because they do things differently to you.
- Don't stick to the rules always, look at the performance and the results not the clock.

CHAPTER NINE

How to be Paid to Travel

- Connecting the Dots
- Values Test
- Road Blocks
- Formula for Success

"Coming together is a beginning;
keeping together is progress;
Working together is success."

Henry Ford

CHAPTER NINE

How to be Paid to Travel

Connecting the Dots

There are many ways to be paid to travel, as you will know having read the preceding chapters and followed the success stories of those featured in this book.

Now the question is, how can you do it too?

Answer: by connecting the dots.

What are the common traits these billionaires, celebrities and success stories share? In reviewing each of the previous chapters we see the key takeaways at the end of each chapter where the same traits are showing up in those interviewed. What they share in common and what they identify as their keys to success.

Suggestion: As you cast your eyes over this list, place a tick next to those traits you believe you already have certainty with and a question mark next to those you are not certain about and would possibly need some guidance and assistance with.

Connecting the Dots:

- Do what you love and love what you do
- Be focused, creative, imaginative, competitive and determined
- Establish your highest values this is what drives your passion
- Start with a clear dream stay focused and passionate

- Overcome your limiting beliefs and roadblocks that are holding you back
- Be flexible and open to change
- Don't wait for a crisis to hit in order to effect change
- Make your vacation your vocation
- Set goals and take small actions steps to achieve them one step at a time
- Push your own boundaries, put your goals in writing
- Delegate other tasks and focus on what is most important to you
- Make personal development a priority and invest in yourself
- Be grateful for all you have in life and more will flow to you
- You don't have to be perfect you just have to start. Take Action
- Be persistent and consistent
- Reward and recognise good work, value the people you work with
- There are no mistakes or failures only opportunities to do better
- Have faith in yourself build your self-confidence, focus on what you are good at
- Stay present and if something is not working, find another way
- Get out of your comfort zone and get comfortable being uncomfortable
- Take a leap of faith and cultivate your self-respect
- In times of doubt look back at how far you've come and keep going!
- Recognise talent and mentor those around you
- No matter how far up the food chain you are, find a mentor to work with
- If you never ask you will never receive
- Be an empire-builder, have a vision bigger than yourself.

The next question to ask and answer is: How do I find out what my passion is?

Take the Values test[1] by asking and answering a series of questions listed below, look at your life, what you surround yourself with, what is in your immediate home, office and environment and in all seven areas of your life.

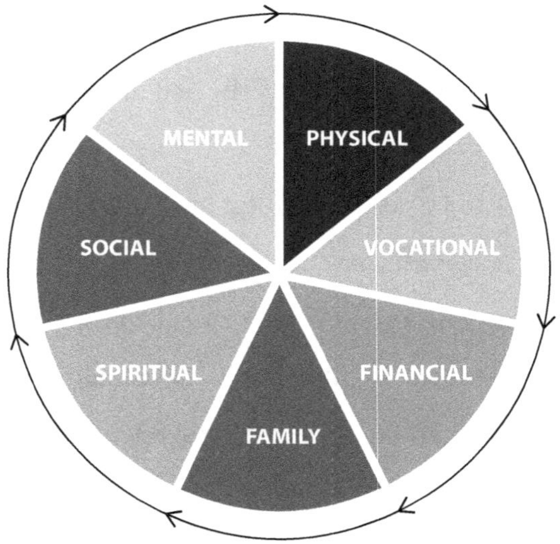

1. How do you fill your space?
2. How do you spend your time?
3. How do you spend your energy?
4. How do you spend your money?
5. Where are you most organised?

1 T*he Values Factor* by Dr John DeMartini also available online https://drdemartini.com/values/login

6. Where are you most disciplined?

7. What do you think about most of the time?

8. What do you visualise most?

9. What do you talk to yourself about?

10. What do you talk with others about?

11. What do you respond to?

12. What are your goals and or ambitions?

13. What do you love most to learn about and read about?

Ask yourself each question in turn, and then ask the same question as to how it relates to each area in your life for example: How do I fill my space with things that relate to my social life, my mental thoughts, my vocational occupation and keep going through all seven areas of your life.

Next do the same again with Question 2: How do I spend my time? In social settings, what do I think about most of the time? How do I spend my time in my career or vocation? Keep going through all seven areas of your life.

Once you have built up a profile of your interior self and brought this into your conscious awareness, you will see a repeating pattern emerge. The same words will keep showing up.

Let's take a look at these repeating words and see how they all fit together, like puzzle pieces, to answer the most important question: **What are your highest values?**

For me it was travel, researching, writing and teaching but only after the third attempt. Remember don't give up!

Common Fears and Road Blocks

Next question to ask is, what are my fears and road blocks? What do I need to face and overcome in order to succeed?

Fear is debilitating and paralysing. It holds us captive and prevents us taking the necessary steps to grow and move forward. What is fear? Below are two acronyms for FEAR. Which applies to you? Be honest, do you cut and run or do you reframe your fear in order to move past it?

Fears and road blocks that hold you back:

F... **k	**F**... false
E... everything	**E**... evidence
A... and	**A**... appearing
R... run	**R**... real

Go down this list and place a tick alongside any that resonate with you.

This list was gathered from an online survey of aspiring business owners and budding entrepreneurs. Some fears may surprise you. FEAR is not rational but irrational and based in hidden unconscious beliefs. Often these beliefs stem from early childhood experiences. So what do you FEAR? And how do you respond to your fears? What could possibly be a roadblock to you living your dream? Until you bring them into your conscious awareness they will remain a hidden barrier.

- Fear of success
- Fear of overwhelmed by time and effort required to see my vision through
- Fear of change and the unknown
- Fear I'm not good enough

- Fearful of people (hiding behind technology)
- Fear steps I take will waste my time and money
- Fear of picking up the phone
- Fear I won't realise my full potential and play a smaller game
- Fear of being mediocre
- Fear of distractions – putting others first (family)
- Fear of not being able to effectively delegate
- Fear of litigation
- Fear of public speaking
- Fear it's not going to be perfect
- Fear if I quit my day job I'll be broke
- Fear I'll be unable to nail my niche
- No clue about social media
- Great idea, no experience – don't know where to start
- Fear of putting myself out there
- Fear of not being organised
- Fear people will turn against me
- Fear of making a mistake
- Fear I'll fail and lose my family
- Fear I'll overthink it and talk myself out of taking action
- Fear of stepping out of my comfort zone into the unknown
- Fear of being seen and valued
- Fear I lack what is needed to be successful
- Fear I lack the X factor

- Fear of talking to new people and telling them about my business
- Biggest roadblock is myself, and not changing what I'm doing
- Fear of letting go and seeing where it can take me
- Fear I wont make enough money and will be forced back to my job
- Biggest challenge has been sorting out my marketing plan
- Lack of guidance and instruction
- Fear of irrelevance – how can I genuinely say my services are better than others?
- Finding my promotional story that I can believe in
- Fear I've left it too late
- Solving the mystery of where are my customers
- Fear of disappointing others
- Fear I don't know enough
- Fear I'll be exposed as not being an expert in my field
- Fear I cannot manage my time effectively and will be overwhelmed
- Fear of failing due to lack of support and guidance
- Fear I'd fail when asked a question (not expert enough)
- Fear of feeling free to be successful, imaginative and unstoppable
- Fear of rejection
- Fear of judgment from peers
- Fear I'll grow too fast and not have time to train talent so I will fail
- Fear of success taking time away from family
- Fear I don't have pieces of paper to legitimise what I know
- No time, not enough cash, no confidence
- Fear I'll succeed and it wont make me happy

- Fear I'll not be able to recreate my former success a second time
- Lack of capital and knowledge
- Fear being able to convince others to buy my vision and products

All your fears and limiting beliefs can be dissolved with some help, education and guidance using the collapse system or some form of therapy. Generally these blocks fall into these broad categories:

1. Lack of confidence and self-belief – Mindset
2. Lack of planning and step by step goal setting – Create a Vision Plan
3. Lack of marketing and sales skill – Service versus Sales
4. Lack of knowledge and guidance – Education and Facilitation
5. Lack of Leadership – Mentoring

Formula for Success

"The masses wait to see before they will believe. The master believes and then watches it unfold and materialise. The master co-creates with the universe the life of his/her dreams. With every thought in every moment of every day we create our own reality"

Merrian Styles

Mindset

The distinguishing feature of geniuses is their passion and dedication to their craft, and particularly, the way in which they identify, confront, and take pains to remedy their weaknesses (Good, Rattan, and Dweck, 2008).

In other words, it's not what you are born with that matters; it's your mindset that matters.

So do you have a growth mindset or a fixed mindset? Are you open to change and growth? Or are you stuck in your ways and fixed in your ideas? The fastest way to find out is go to the URL below and take the online test developed by Carol S. Dweck, Ph.D., who is one of the world's leading researchers in the field of motivation and is the Lewis and Virginia Eaton Professor of Psychology at Stanford University.

http://www.mindsetonline.com/testyourmindset/step1.php

Once you've taken the test and established how growth orientated or fixed orientated you are, you know where to begin to shift and to work with or change your mindset.

Meditation and Focus

Many of those interviewed including myself have used meditation and other practices to still the mind as a way of going within and listening to our intuitive inner voice. Others have said it was their ability to get really focused on what was important to them that they attributed to their success. Whatever way you choose, be mindful of your self-talk. Observe what you are saying to yourself, and actively decide to change the chatter by learning to quiet your mind in order for your inner voice to be heard. It's that ability to focus your attention and reframe your focus that will guarantee your success. Where you place your attention that is what you will attract.

What you practice you grow.

Place your focus on feeling good now, and the universe will deliver you more to feel good about. For recommendations on meditation courses and guided meditations go to www.merrianstyles.com

Creating a Vision – The Dream is in the Detail

To be a success, you must be willing to do whatever it takes to achieve your dreams, but there's always a price to pay. There are no free rides you have to be prepared to take action and sometimes that feels metaphorically a little like leaping off a cliff. It requires a leap of faith.

- If you get absolutely crystal clear on exactly what you love, and you cannot see anything but that, then it's almost impossible for you not to get it.
- If you know that no matter what happens, your life is serving your dreams, then nothing can stop you. The minute you truly commit to your dream, watch the universe immediately bring you the nourishment and the challenges necessary to fulfil it.

> *"Be prepared to get comfortable with being uncomfortable."*
>
> **Merrian Styles**

Secrets of an Inspired Life

- The quality of your life is determined by the quality of the questions you ask.
- Even when you are not inspired and consciously following your vision, you still play a part in the divine order. If you feel like you're off-purpose, refocus and reframe your attention back on your vision to get back on track and take the next inspired action step. Remember you are the creator of your own reality.

EXERCISE

Create the life you love:

1. Every day, sit for a moment (or at least 10 minutes) in silent meditation and concentrate on exactly what you would love to create in your life. Imagine every detail you can, and then even more. Let your imagination be real enough to come true, yet ideal enough to inspire and stretch you.

2. Write down all that you can imagine, and begin formulating your goals. Writing down your dreams helps them come true, so include as many details as possible. The more real it FEELS the faster it will manifest.

3. Every day, take at least one action step towards making your dreams come true. What you move towards moves towards you. Think of it as an investment in the universal bank of creation. For all the energy deposits you make, the universe reciprocates with an equal or greater energy deposit.

4. Keep a record of every synchronous, goal-aligned event that occurs; they fill your life when you stop to acknowledge them. Acknowledging your progress is a statement of awareness and gratitude to the universe. Write down all the events that come true for you each day, demonstrating that you are moving in the direction of your dreams.

5. Keep refining your goals, getting clearer and clearer with each passing day.

6. As you fulfil your goals, be sure to add new ones, always with your highest values and your purpose in mind.

EXERCISE (continued)

7. Maintain a gratitude journal. Be thankful for all you have in your life now, and for every supportive or challenging event that provides feedback and fulfilment on your journey to actualising your dreams. Celebrate your successes however small.

"Your vision will become clearer, only when you look into your heart. Who looks outside, dreams. Who looks inside awakens."

Carl Jung

The Energy Equation

The universal law of polarity; everybody has two sides. If you are honest, you'll see that you are both saint and sinner, virtuous and vicious. So when someone accuses you of something, don't waste time defending yourself. Instead, admit that you are in fact the possessor that trait. Not only are you the possessor of that trait but your accuser is also.

If it hurts you to hear it, this means you haven't yet seen how that quality serves you or others and you are judging yourself. The gift is to wake you up to another part of yourself that you haven't yet loved and to own that part. Whatever arises, love that. Tell yourself every day all is well and take a deep life giving breath.

"Whatever you do, you do to yourself.
To judge others only compounds your own faults."

Buddha

- People who try to be positive to everybody, at home and in the world, end up negating themselves.
- If you try to put on a façade for the world about how positive an upbeat you are, there will be chaos in your private life or your personal health.
- Tragedy heals self-righteous people; it humbles them back down into their hearts. Comedy heals self-erroneous people by lifting them back up into their heart.

"The longer I stayed positive, the more something would blow, and I'd get really negative, either to myself or someone else. I noticed that the more I tried to put on the façade of being positive, the more I'd beat myself up inside. No matter what I did, I couldn't get rid of my negative side".

Dr John Demartini

While the universal law of polarity acknowledges the existence of both our positive and negative sides, and while we cannot deny the existence of our negative aspects, when it comes to self talk, we can CHOOSE to focus and refocus, our attention on what we value and love. In this way we attract more of what FEELS good now, into our lives. This is the universal law of attraction.

Q: If everything you did, said and thought was broadcast 24 hours a day on the eternity channel, and everyone knew everything there was to know about you, could you love yourself?

Mastery is the ability to take your private life public. If you can take the private things you don't like about yourself and embrace them to the point where it doesn't matter if people find out about them or not, then you love yourself. When you love yourself, people can't trigger you, but they will automatically attack you in whatever areas you judge yourself. Where you judge yourself can also be heard as your negative self talk, so be mindful of what you are saying externally and internally. Remember your outer reality is a reflection of your inner world.

When you give yourself permission to be fully human and fallible, you approach the divine. There is perfection in being imperfect.

EXERCISE

How to always feel good no matter where you find yourself living. Look for the differences between others and us. Now reverse that. Look for the similarities between others and us. Sit in a public place where you can watch the world go by, and start identifying yourself in the people you see. Look from person to person quickly and whatever trait that stands out about them, ask yourself if you have the same quality. Find out where and when you're exactly like them. Own the trait.

As you improve you will be able to find yourself in anyone and everyone. Celebrate the differences and rejoice in the similarities. Feel good now and as often as possible and observe as the universe gives you the life you dream of living.

Fail to Plan, Plan to Fail

- The Divine is in the details. An inspired vision isn't just some vague perception; it must be extremely clear and detailed.
- In the creation process, there needs to be balance between MAKING things happen and ALLOWING things to happen. It's wise to have a laid-out plan, but not one so rigid that you can't allow refinement or adaption. Be flexible and adaptable. Excavate, evaluate and refine.
- The purpose of a plan is not to make it the ONLY way, but to ALLOW your mind to see it clearly enough to erase all fear and doubts and ALLOW it to materialise then you attract what you envision or an even better alternative appears usually from somewhere totally unexpected.
- If you set a goal with your self-righteous persona, you're going to get burned out attempting to accomplish it. If you set a goal with your self-erroneous persona, you won't be motivated and you'll be bored. Inspiring visions that are crystal clear can be manifested. DON'T get elated or depressed about them; you just keep working away until they materialise. You MUST take inspired action for this to happen.
- People who study only practical matters don't develop a broad enough vision to extend beyond themselves. They must be stretched and made uncomfortable to get beyond their comfort zone in order to achieve and succeed.

> *"The real voyage of discovery consists not in seeking new landscapes, but in having new eyes."*
>
> **Marcel Proust**

- Plan to live your life fully, until the moment you stop breathing, being productive and doing something that truly inspires you and serves others.

- The most magnificent thing in life is to be able to get up every morning and do what you love and love what you do, to be well paid and inspired to do it. **Make your vacation your vocation**.
- Most people are too busy to take the time to plan, and they are too distracted by low-priority actions instead of committing themselves to high-priority dreams.
- You are the author of your own life.
- Whoever has the most certainty wins.
- Be the one that is certain.
- People follow confidence, be an inspired leader.

Service and Marketing

The universal law of reciprocity states: that whatever is sent out into the cosmos – what quantum physics refers to as "The Unified Field", and what I personally choose to refer to as "The Infinite Field Of Possibility", in the way of energy or vibration through the resonance of your thoughts, emotions and actions – will manifest outcomes in the physical world, physical outcomes that unfold in your life based on whatever is broadcast out through those thoughts, emotions and actions.

The movie *The Secret* featured many transformational speakers and authors include Dr John Demartini. Most of them draw on ancient knowledge and wisdom. It's no secret the teachings contained in the book and movie, have been around for centuries. The difference with *The Secret* was marketing.

Most people don't understand marketing. Briefly however, in order to receive you need to give, give and give a minimum of three times before you can expect to receive something in return. **This is the law of reciprocity in action.** You need to broadcast out into the universe resonating thoughts and actions that attract reciprocal energetic manifestations in the physical world.

Think of sales as providing service. Consider meeting a prospective client as though you are going on a date. On the first date, you never expect to receive a marriage proposal, do you? So why would you expect a sale on your first meeting? Court your client, woo them with your gifts and talents, and give them a taste of what you have to offer. On social media, up to 15 touch points of engagement are needed before you ask for anything in return.

Build TRUST. Here are 12 things that influence people's decision to trust you.

- Confidence
- Congruence
- Professional appearance
- Communicate your good intentions upfront
- Integrity – make promises and requests and make sure you deliver
- Actively listen to keywords and mirror them back
- Express your concerns and fears
- Discuss potential future problems or issues
- Provide accurate information avoid ball-parking
- Negotiate for abundance by painting a win–win scenario
- Use rapport techniques to establish you are on the same side
- Reveal something personal about yourself

Connection, credibility and trust are the foundations for exploring if a potential client is a good fit or not. Add a touch of urgency to the mix, spell out the vision clearly for all to see, creating a win–win for all parties and then make a request but not before.

Blueprint of Creation

> *"If you believe in a divine creator, work with him/her. If you do not, become one."*
>
> **Merrian Styles**

Overcoming Objections. There are many layers of excuses to the question "why are you not self-actualising your life and living your dream?" Each answer is based in fear and or guilt.

I am NOT living my dream life because:

- I *desire* to lose 10 kg of fat first.
- I *want* to pay off my debts first.
- I *need* to complete my education first.
- I *ought* to spend my time donating my time to charity first.
- I *have* to raise my family first.

None of these are necessarily true. They are all excuses we tell ourselves for not doing what we love. Anyone with an **unshakable belief in themselves**, and an absolute certainty about what they want to do, could lose everything and still have the courage and conviction to create it all again. The question is, do you?

To materialise your dreams, you must consistently take two action steps:

1. Define your dreams. If you don't or can't define them, don't expect to have them.
2. Ask yourself what's in the way of those dreams? If you find yourself making excuses know you can dissolve them by using the **collapse system**[2].

2 Collapse system is one where you balance the benefits against the challenges until there is a collapse of polarised views and perceptions. Once equilibrium is reached the resistance collapses. www.merrianstyles.com/workshops-and-seminars.html

If you procrastinate, look at these three areas:

- an undetailed goal,
- a lopsided perception,
- a dream that isn't linked or aligned to your highest values.

NEXT: balance your perceptions. Detail your goals, break each goal into bite-size steps, and link them to your highest values and how those steps will serve your progress to achieving that goal.

Self-actualization requires no excuses. People use excuses to justify why they are not doing what they love. Procrastination = avoidance. Ask yourself: Why am I avoiding taking the next step? What is holding me back? Invariably your answer will be based in fear or guilt.

Know that giving and taking are two sides of the one coin and both are necessary to maintain equilibrium. Balance is everything.

Become aware and awake to your own and others hidden agendas.

- Self-mastery requires the law of fair exchange to operate. Following the Greek proverb:

> *"Payment is due when services are rendered."*

- If you receive a large inheritance and you don't know what you've done to deserve it, some equilibrating force is likely to reduce that amount to exactly what you feel you've earned. It will quickly reveal how you VALUE yourself. This phenomenon is often seen in lottery winners who within two years have lost the entire fortune they won and are back doing the job they recently left following their windfall.
- To equilibrate your perception and feel that there has been fair exchange, you'd be wise to find out what you did to deserve what you have received. To see what VALUE you bring to the world.

- The universe is asking you "what is your value?" and waiting patiently until you finally wake up to it.

> *"I'm in the right place at the right time to meet the right people and make the right choices."*
>
> **Merrian Styles**

If you experience any doubts, fill your mind with high-priority thoughts, and take high-priority actions steps. Fill your day with the things you love, and watch what happens.

Be thankful for what you have and what you love.

- Purpose + Thought + Vision + Affirmation + Feeling + writing things down in space and time + taking action with energy + gratitude manifests your heart's desires.
- What if it takes two or three years to manifest your dreams? So what? What else would you do with those years? Waft around in uncertainty?
- What if at the end of your life you are asked "Did you do everything you could with everything you were given?" What do you want to answer?
- Know how to eat an elephant? One bite at a time. Take the first bite.

Completion: Full Circle

> *"Your mind dictates your destiny and your most dominant thought determines your world. Don't just repeat the words I've given you; become them. Say them as if your life depended on them."*
>
> **Paul Bragg**

- Ancient wisdom dictates that if you don't pass on your light to another, you won't receive greater light. Whatever you would love to master, pass it on like a torch. If you help others achieve what they would love to achieve in life, you'll be more enabled to achieve what you desire and love in your life.

"To those who believe, no proof is necessary. To those who don't believe, no proof is possible."

Stuart Chase

- Waste no words on those who seek not. Sometimes silence is more powerful than speech. Be wise in your selection of torchbearers.
- The quicker you gather information and the faster you give it to others, the more you remember.
- The more time that lapses between receiving and broadcasting, the less you retain and the less certain you become. If you would love to have a photographic mind, give out immediately what you've taken in.

"Do not seek to follow in the footsteps of the wise men of old. Seek what they sought."

Matsuo Menefusa

It doesn't matter if you are afraid. Everybody who ever did anything extraordinary was frightened at times. If you have great fear, you also have great courage, for they remain in equal proportions; and both are necessary for us to evolve and grow. Have an unshakable belief in yourself above all else.

"Many of life's failures are people who did not realise how close they were to success when they gave up."

Thomas Edison

Never Give Up!

ABOUT THE AUTHOR

Merrian Styles

Author, Marketing Consultant, Change Facilitator, and Public Speaker

Merrian started her career as an article clerk in North Sydney, before setting out on an intrepid journey of work that took her to all parts of the globe. Travel is a great teacher. Merrian is an author, change facilitator, marketing consultant, and public speaker.

In her marketing consultant role, she produces dynamic marketing programs for her clients. As a change facilitator, she has more than two decades of experience, as the Expat Expert, her presentations and inspirational workshops draw on a colourful life packed with great stories, each story brings with it a valuable lesson.

A graduate of Oxford Brookes University and the University of Western Australia, she also holds certificates in acupressure, Tai Chi, and Pa Kua Tai Chi Chuan and is an advanced open-water diver.

During her 20-year professional career, Merrian has held the position of company director at several major companies, including Advanced Techtonics Pty Ltd, DFSS, Specialist Drilling Fluids Services, and Bespoke Enterprises. Some of the companies she has worked with include Chevron, Woodside, Exxon Mobile, ENI, Shell Inpex MI, HOEC, and Baker Hughes International.

She lists building a mobile mud plant for Chevron's Barrow Island Exploration project as her biggest achievement. Merrian took an engineer's design for the mobile plant to Singapore and Vietnam and built 12 x 40 foot containers that linked together with couplings to create a portable mobile plant for the drilling section of the project. Her work earned her the nickname 'Tank Lady'. At the end of the project, she sold the plant to Baker Hughes International for a substantial profit.

Merrian's professional and social associations include the Overseas Women's Club of Madras, the Maadi British Association of Cairo, Friends of the Street Children of Cairo, Friends of Forrest Park, and the Berrimah Riding Club. Her other interests include scuba diving, open-water diving, as well as salsa and bachata dancing. She is also a mentor for the Just Start program which teaches high school students how to start their own business.

She has lived, travelled, and worked throughout the UK, Israel, Greece, Singapore, Malaysia, Thailand, Saudi Arabia, Pakistan, Indonesia, Vietnam, Philippines, India, Egypt, the United States, Bermuda, Kenya, Bahrain, Dubai, Abu Dhabi, United Arab Emirates, Tibet, Nepal, Jordan, New Zealand, France, Belgium, Germany, Netherlands, Italy, Spain, Portugal, Poland, Czech Republic, Austria, Hungry and Monaco.

Merrian Styles is the author of *Taking Off* and lives in Western Australia.

RESOURCES

Survival Kit and Moving Kit:

For free resources go to: http://www.merrianstyles.com/free-resources.html

Ongoing Support:

For free resources go to: http://www.merrianstyles.com/free-resources.html

The seven part series of Taking Off Fun-shops available
www.merrianstyles/workshops-and-seminars.html

1. Flight preparation – What you need to know.
2. Checklist – What you need to ask.
3. Prepare for take-off – Why are you in a holding pattern?
4. Full throttle and lift off – How you shift gears and rev up!
5. Inflight entertainment – Why you need fun.
6. Prepare for landing – How to make adjustments.
7. Touch down – The adventure begins!

For a Media Kit or more information email: info@merrianstyles.com or visit www.merrianstyles.com

Recommended Resources:

www.merrianstyles.com

www.natashazuvela.com

http://www.confidenceoncamera.com.au/

https://changinghabits.com.au/

www.DrDemartini.com

https://drdemartini.com/values/login

www.krugercowne.com

https://www.oneyoungworld.com

https://www.oneyoungworld.com/news-item/rising-star-programme-finalists-announced

https://www.steelheels.com.au/

https://www.studentuniverse.com/

www.manifestingmatisse.com

http://ww1.mastermanifestors.com/

http://www.mindsetonline.com/testyourmindset/step1.php

https://www4.esu.edu/academics/enrichment_learning/documents/pdf/developing_growth_mindset.pdf

www.HowToBePaidToTravel.com

www.TakingOffTheBook.com

www.ingramcontent.com/pod-product-compliance
Lightning Source LLC
LaVergne TN
LVHW010059110826
845155LV00028B/410

* 9 7 8 1 9 2 5 2 8 8 7 0 4 *